D0367448

We, The
BRIDE

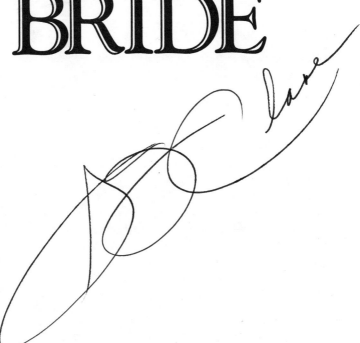

We, The
BRIDE

SISTER FRANCIS CLARE SSND

New Leaf
Press

1st Printing, Nov. 1990
2nd Printing, Jan 1991 (Revised)

Scripture quotations are from the New American Bible, unless otherwise stated.
Copyright 1970 by The World Publishing Company.

Copyright 1990, by New Leaf Press, Inc. All rights reserved. Printed in the United States of America. No part of this book may be used or reproduced in any manner whatsoever without written permission of the publisher except in the case of brief quotations in articles and reviews. For information write: New Leaf Press, Inc., P.O. Box 311, Green Forest, AR 72638.

Typesetting by: Type-O-Graphics, Springfield, MO

Library of Congress Catalog Number: 90-63012
ISBN: 0-89221-187-3

Color Photos - Tony Cilento, Milwaukee, WI
Back Cover Photo - Walter J. Roob
                    Milwaukee, WI

DEDICATION

To Jesus, the Bridegroom,
and to all of God's people whom I have
come to know and to love as the Bride of Jesus.

ACKNOWLEDGEMENTS

I wish to express appreciation to all who have inspired, prayed for, encouraged, or assisted me in any way in the birthing of We, The Bride.

TABLE OF CONTENTS

INTRODUCTION

We, the people of God, we, who are called by His name, are called to be part of the greatest love affair in all of history. Jesus the King of kings, the Lord of lords, the Master of heaven and earth, is out to court His bride and we are the Bride He is courting. He is calling each one of us by name Robert, Susan, John, Marie, Philip, Nora, Michael. He is calling us from the market places of our lives, from the highways, the byways, the places that we have hid from Him. He is calling us because He is madly in love with us and He would woo us into that place where we can say, "I'm in love with my God, my God's in love with me!"

Every other love affair in the course of history has been but a shadow of what this is, the love between my God and me—the love story that reached its heights on Calvary, that was planned in the heart of our God from all eternity. The mystery of this love story to a large extent has been hidden from ages and generations past, but now it is being revealed and popularized across the face of the earth.

We are being called to discover God's bridal love for us and to pledge our "first love" or bridal love for Him. Ultimately there is only one love affair and that is with our God.

FOREWORD

We are called to be members of God's family. In striving to appreciate the beauty of this relationship we speak in human, even endearing terms. In an age when many find it difficult to believe in God, Sister Francis Clare highlights the joy of living in intimacy with God. She shares here bridal conversations that we might hear God speak to us:

Indeed, I am with you
but you will never know
    the power of this "with-ness"
unless you are also with Me.
This is a daily, hourly, minutely choice
    you must take time to be with Me.
I want to walk with you.
    Choose to walk with Me.
I want to talk with you.
    Choose to talk with Me.
I want to be one with you.
    Choose to be one with Me.
              We, The Bride p. 143.

Sister's reflections help us to see anew the special beauty of being Bride and to appreciate again God's tremendous desire to be one with us, His beloved.

Taste and see.

Most Reverend William E. Franklin
Auxiliary Bishop of Dubuque, Iowa

CHAPTER ONE

THE STORY BEHIND THE STORY

"Tell Sister Fran that she is to write another book and it is to be themed the Bride." This word came to Dr. Bernie Klamecki, president of the Association of Christian Therapists, in his personal prayer time, after I had been sharing with him some of the amazing things that happen to people who make retreats on God's bridal Love for them.

"Another book! God, I am not over the labor pains from the last one," was my first voiced gut response.

Later that day I repented enough to pray, "God, if that is really true, how come You told Bernie and not me?"

"Because you would never have believed it. It is true all right and and the title is *We, The Bride*."

There was no mistaking what I had heard. That was seven years ago when the ink was hardly dry on the first printing of *Your Move, God*.

Though I never questioned the call to write, I did little or nothing about it for at least three years. Then one day during spiritual direction I was moved to ask my director, "Why don't you ask God if I am really called to write again, and what I am supposed to be doing about it?"

There was the typical Jesuit pause for discernment before Father Bill Kurz shared, "What comes to me is this, when God gave you your last book, God just gave it to you and said, 'Now live it.' For the next one God is saying, 'First you live it and then I'll give it.'"

"'First you live it and then I'll give it.' That is a great one liner," I mused.

Several months slipped by, during which I shared God's great one-liner with friends in response to: "How are you doing, Fran? Any progress on your book?"

Finally, a half year later, when I was away for my yearly retreat, I began to question God: "How am I doing? What is the first thing You want me to do?"

"Repent!" The response was quick. And it was clear. "Repent for sharing My one-liner with a lot of whomsoevers and never once asking Me, 'What do You mean by "Live it so You can give it!"'"

"Oh God, I repent. I really do. I know now that I truly 'blew it.' I should have asked. I could have asked. I am asking right now. Forgive me, precious Jesus, for never once asking what You meant by 'Live it so You can give it.' I really want to know, so that I can do just that beginning with this retreat."

When I got quiet enough on the inside I heard, "First, I want you to love the Bride that you are. Then I want you to love the Bride that is the community you live with, the Bride that is the larger Notre Dame community, the Bride that is your church, the Bride that is the churches of all denominations, the Bride that is unchurched, the Bride that is the world."

On the inside I was experiencing skid marks all over the King's highway. "God, I can't love that much! Do You realize how unlovely the Bride is—beginning with me?''

Living in an experiential, intentional Charismatic community of School Sisters of Notre Dame's (SSND's) is an unparalleled grace, one in which we not only came to know God but we came to know each other. We came to see with the eyes of the heart both how lovely and how unlovely we are.

''God, I can't love Your Bride the way You want, with the height, the length, the depth, the vastness You expect. It is too much! I am just beginning to get in touch with all the reasons why I can't even love myself on the level that You are asking.''

As I look back, I realize this was one of those God-wrestling retreats that tested every spiritual muscle in my being. What I did not know then was how strongly my resistance to love was rooted in the need for the healing of my psyche, the need for dealing with buried anger.

Only later I remembered that for years whenever my friend, Fr. Bob, would pray for me, he would invariably end his prayer with, ''Sister Fran, you have a lot of buried anger.''

For years, at least ten, my response was, ''Buried anger, huh! As long as it is buried, fine! Just don't let it pop up and hurt anyone or destroy me!''

Something new was happening in this retreat as I began to pray: ''God, if I am to love the Bride I am and to write for the Bride that is Your people, perhaps it is time for me to do something about that buried anger that could be blocking my loving. Show me what I am to do and when.''

''God, show me what and when!''

The answer came in prayer. ''You need to be tested for those buried angers,'' my MA background in psychology prompted. ''If they find anything,'' I mused, ''I will begin with a few sessions of professional help. Then I will pursue some healing prayer for a fast miraculous healing,'' my MA (miracles abounding) background in ministry quickly jumped in. "Then I will be ready to write, *We, The Bride.*"

Needless to say it did not quite work that way. The results of several hours of MMPI (Minnesota Multi Phasic Inventory) testing showed a lot of buried anger.

The direction was right. The speed was different. I came to know the truth of a favorite maxim of the foundress of our Order, Blessed Theresa of Jesus Gerhardinger, "All the works of God proceed slowly and with pain, therefore the roots are sturdier and the flowers lovelier."

Not without pain and a sizable backlog of my own personal misgiving, I began the sessions with Dr. Madeline Fronke, a clinical psychologist, who is a Spirit-filled nun. My opening statement to Dr. Fronke was: "I like the me I am, but I am not sure that I will like the me I become when you are finished with me."

My inability to trust began showing up all over the place. To my dismay and amazement, I discovered that it was not limited to people but was strongly rooted in my subconscious relationship with God. In the middle of the night I would awaken to the sound of my own voice declaring, "God, I can't even trust You."

Yet somehow I knew as I launched into the deep of weekly therapy sessions, that I was entrusting my earthen vessel, my cracked pottery, not just to Dr. Fronke's skills and charism but to the Divine Potter.

Weekly I was led to just the right word from Scripture to trigger a new walk, jump, leap into my past and to discover that my God was ready to walk, jump, leap the path with me.

Even though I could sense God's nearness in this new adventure, therapy was by no means easy for me. Shifting my psychological gears left me feeling more like the Gordian knot than the full speed ahead Interstate driver that I was used to. My spiritual director of the '70s used to declare: "Sister Fran, when you come in, I feel like I have just turned off a side road to the interstate."

A part of me felt like I was back on one of those side roads digging my heels into the dust praying: "Oh God, this is some Herculean task to dig up my past, but if You come through it with me, I am willing to make the journey."

God was willing.

Lights began to go on and I began to have some enthusiasm for what had seemed to me incredibly vague and utterly impossible. I began to see that it was all right for me to take off my rose-colored glasses and to see my world as it truly exists.

It really surprises me to share this part of my world with your world, to let go of some of the WOW in my life and to share with you some of the long buried OW. As I do, I say, "Take courage, Bride, out there with your combat boots on. We all have an enormous battle to fight but Jesus our Bridegroom will go to battle for us."

God says to us as to King Jehoshaphat: "Do not fear or lose heart at the sight of this vast multitude, for the battle is not yours but God's. Take your place, stand firm, and see how the Lord will be with you to deliver you" (2 Chron. 20:15-17).

Looking over my prayer journals of the past ten years, I discovered how wonderfully faithful God has been even when I have not been that faithful. I saw God stick with me through thick and thin, for better or for worse, for richer for poorer, in good times and in bad. What a Bridegroom!

One of the favorite names God calls me is, "Franny, My fun-bride." I have asked Jesus, "What makes me Your fun-bride?"

"You are so open to try the untried, the down-to-earth, the off-the-clouds, that I can suggest almost anything and you are there to agree. No, it has never been tried, but what is keeping us from being the first?"

Seven years ago when we were discerning the move to Milwaukee into an about-to-be-formed SSND charismatic community I was awakened in the night with God speaking, "This is it. This is what I have formed you for. This is what I am calling you to, and if you think it is going to be fun for you—you ought to know the fun it is going to be for Me. Fun for the Father! Fun for the Son! Fun for the Holy Spirit!"

This was the first of many prophetic words that brought Sisters Josephe Marie Flynn, Jean Andrew Dickmann, Kathy Van Hulst, Clare Rushlow, Carleen Peters, and myself to eventually seek permission to set up a Charismatic SSND community at St. Rita's, Milwaukee. Another word that inspired us was from Cada's book, *Shaping the Coming Age of Religious Life*: "It is not enough for individual Religious to experience conversion, when Religious with the same kind of conversion experience come together, then the community will be converted."

God's promise to us was: "I will lead you step by step." God led. We came to know step by step what it is to live as a charismatic community under the Lordship of Jesus, fully open with one another, ministering to each other and others in the full power of the Charismatic gifts. It was fun for us and fun for God.

With each of us in a different kind of ministry it might have been easy to lose our perspective. Lest that happen the Lord came quickly to our rescue with this banner line: **"What happens among you is more important than what you accomplish."**

In addition to the fun, we experienced the hard, hard times that come from being radically open to growth in wholeness and in holiness. Not without pain we struggled through old patterns and pioneered new paths. At one of our meetings Josephe came up with this definition of community: "Community is a safe place in which to share your pain."

Pain can come from varied backgrounds, from the fact that we are very different from one another. On one of the early days before our coming together as we were praying about how unlike we are, we received the imagery of a tunnel. Josephe was in the middle of the tunnel shouting: "C'mon Jeanie, let's go! Let's go! There are wonderful things ahead down this tunnel. What's keeping you?"

"Oh, but Josephe, do you hear that echo! Have you seen the exquisite cobwebs here at the entrance to the tunnel? The patterns are out of this world! If only I had a camera!"

"C'mon Jeanie, let's go! Let's go! Don't you know what time it is?"

"Where's Fran?"

"Are you kidding? She's way ahead of us. Fran is drilling the tunnel!"

In our years together we have done a lot of praying and some goal-setting to help bring about a unity in our diversity. The first year we agreed on this prayer goal, "God, give us a common mind."

The next year we changed to, "God, give us a common heart."

The following year we advanced to, "Jesus, help us to reverence one another as You reverence us." From year to year we experienced quantum leaps of growth. On one of our end-of-the year evaluation days on living religious life I recall stating, "I believe I have made more progress in the last six years than in the first thirty-six."

After saying it, I questioned, "Did I say that?" I proceeded to answer my own question, "I surely did, and I believe it is the humble truth—more progress in the last six years than in the first thirty-six!"

This past year we bonded with the prayer, "Jesus, convert us from lives of pressure to lives of simplicity and balance." Conversions are never easy. We have graced our kitchen with the poster, "God made all of us saints. He just is not finished with us yet."

I know that God is not nearly finished with me yet, though I have come a long, long way down the road. On one of our preretreat prayer days in Columbus, Ohio when a small group of directors were praying over me, one received the image of a large tipped over bushel basket with a little pair of eyes peering out from under the bushel. He laughed and laughed before he could relate it. When he finally did share the vision he added, "Fran, I think you are still under your bushel."

Then everyone laughed. "If Fran the International is under her bushel, where in the world are the rest of us?"

It was an image I could not forget. If God went to all the trouble to give it, it seemed that I ought to find out more about it.

For nearly a year when people prayed with me and asked, "Sister Fran, what do you want?"

I would say, "I want to know more about that bushel."

Finally one day in response God promised in prophetic word, "I am not only going to take off the bushel but I am going to dismantle it, so that you can never put it on again."

It has happened. It is happening. World, watch out. The Bride is coming out from under her bushel.

CHAPTER TWO

THAT BUSHEL AGAIN

"Bob, have I got good news for you!" The setting was New Orleans. Weaving in and out among the thousands, I spotted Father Bob DeGrandis at the Leaders' Congress on Evangelism in the spring of 1986.

"Do you remember all the years that you bugged me about my buried angers? I have finally come to believe you, Fr. Bob, and I am doing something about them. It's nothing less than professional help! Now isn't that something!"

"Wonderful! Fran! That is wonderful! Let's slip over to the side for a moment. I believe the Lord wants me to pray with you."

In an instant Bob's hand was on my head and he began praying in a surge of tongues. The next thing I knew he was saying in English, "That's it. I see it all very clearly. You were unwanted in the womb at three months."

Before my mind could register what Bob was saying, I heard, "Oh, I am sorry, Fran, I have to go to dinner." There was a swift charismatic hug and Bob was off in the crowd.

Only when I got to bed that night did I begin to realize that I was absolutely furious on the inside, for what I had been told by Bob. If I ever wanted to give someone with a RC (Roman collar) the biggest kick in the pants he had ever gotten, I wanted to deliver one that night. Something inside of me was outraged! I was furious! In my fury I tossed and turned, sleepless till suddenly the thoughts popped, "What if Bob was right! What if I was unwanted in the womb at three months? What if...."

With that a series of facts flashed through my mind. I was born during the Great Depression. My parents already had five children, all about a year and a half apart. Living on a farm in 1925, my mother could have discovered only after three months that she was pregnant. She could well have said, "No, God, not another one. We can't afford to feed those we have."

With that I must have fallen asleep. By the next morning the trauma was relegated to a back-burner. In my next therapy session I would ask Dr. Fronke what she thought.

She responded, "That could well be the truth. When you were born you hit the deck running with your fist up, thinking, 'If you don't want me, I'll make it on my own.'"

After leaving her office I wrote these reflections in my journal: "If that is really true, my mother better say that she is sorry. And my father better say that he is sorry. And God better say, 'I am sorry.'" I was a bit surprised at what I wrote. But I felt better that I was being real, gutsy real, about a very real gut-something that was happening in me.

As the week went by, something within me was about to panic at being left alone to work through the next step. I needed someone with supernatural gifts, both audio and visual, to help me pray this thing through. I needed both to see and to hear what was going on. So, I phoned my friends, Bernie and Ann Klamecki, both strong in gifts of prophecy and vision. "I need help, some good strong prayer help," I urged.

This was not the first time that Klamecki's front room sofa became my prayer spot to receive whatever God had for me. Without telling Bernie and Ann about Bob's word of knowledge, we began praying in the Spirit for whatever God wanted to show us. To my amazement we had hardly begun to pray when Ann shared, "I have this picture of a little embryo in the womb, about to take off with what seemed like a thousand fighting hands."

Then Ann saw Jesus standing on the side. "Jesus, please comfort that poor little embryo," she prayed. Ann saw Jesus take the struggling fetus from the womb and hold it with utmost tenderness to His heart. As Jesus put it back in the womb it was arrayed in layers of white and stood like a figurine with dancing shoes on a music box.

Then Ann saw my parents. "Your mother is weeping and saying, 'I am so sorry. I didn't mean it.'"

Remembering what I had written I wept, "God, this has to be real. It is just what I asked for in my prayer journal."

Bernie continued, "Your father is saying, 'I am so sorry. I had wanted another boy to help with the farm work!'"

In that moment I realized that not only was I unwanted but I was of the wrong sex. Alone it would have been more than I could handle. My whole inner world was falling apart. For some time Bernie and Ann prayed in the Spirit for the healing of this double rejection. I did not see, but I did feel the presence of Jesus as I prayed along in my prayer language. I desired to receive all the healing my Bridegroom could pour out on His wounded bride.

Before the prayer was over, Bernie received the vision

of a fierce storm rising up out of nowhere. "I am seeing a ferocious storm, Fran. Were you born in a storm?" he asked.

"I was born in winter. But I am sure if there had been a great storm, I would have heard about it in our family tales."

When I shared this with Dr. Fronke she immediately made this interesting connection. "If I had experienced rejection in the womb at three months, I would have fought the birth canal. To be forced from the womb would have been for me another form of rejection."

Painful as all this was, I began to be enthused for the healing I was receiving on many levels. I have always taught that with God there is no such thing as time. There is just the present moment. In this present moment God can heal any other moment in our lives in which we have experienced rejection, abandonment, or trauma.

To receive it in my own psyche on a level that I never dreamed I needed was a new experience. As I persisted in seeking out my continued healing, I sometimes found help in the most unlikely spots. One day while dusting an out-of-the-way shelf I discovered a series of three tapes entitled *Making Peace with Your Past,* by Eddie Ensley. The first tape dealt with your mother, the second with your father, and the third with significant others. Little did I dream, until I took the tapes with me for my yearly retreat, that these would be dynamite in making peace with my past, especially my relationship with my mother.

Against a background of ethereal music in the quiet of my retreat cell, I heard Eddie narrate, "Everyone's parents have failed them. No one's parents have been able to be for them all that they have needed them to be. So in this moment of time picture your mother sitting opposite you in her favorite chair. It does not matter if she is living or dead. Hear her say, 'How do you feel about me?' Do not be too quick to answer. Slowly let your answer rise from some buried out-of-touch place within you. Allow yourself to be very still for as long as it takes, to hear from the deepest part of your being."

For me it took a long, long, long time for any thought to surface.

Finally, almost like a huge hiccup I voiced it, "I don't feel a damn thing!"

Because I do not use that kind of language, I was as surprised at the language as I was at the message. However, the more I pondered what I had heard, the more I knew this was the simple truth—I did not feel a damn thing. For almost fifty years I had not felt anything in relation to my mother. She died of cancer, leaving me when I was a mere thirteen-year-old, without any closure on our relationship. I never had an adult relationship with my mother. There were no feelings.

A flood of tears began to punctuate the hours of that day. Somewhere toward evening I heard this little voice within me state clearly, "But I love her." I knew I had reached the place of my inner child and she was saying the truth as she had experienced it. "But I love her." I was at peace with my journey.

The next day when I returned to the tape, there was a fresh new question to be addressed to me from my mother, "How have I failed you?"

If I had not been warned to be slow to answer, my conscious mind would have been quick to contradict, "But you have never failed me. You were a saint, so you died young. How could anyone as good as you ever fail me?"

Finally, after a long silence, out from under what seemed like a thousand buried cities of pain, I heard my inner child say, "I could never do anything right! I was born left-handed and you forced me to be right-handed."

In that moment an inner earthquake began to set up its tremors. Ever since I did anything on my own, I did it wrong! I was using the wrong hand! Until my mother died when I was in eighth grade, I had to sit next to her at the table to make sure that I ate my food with the proper hand. Teacher after teacher in my grade school disciplined me into writing, drawing, and making the Sign of the Cross with my right hand. Often I wanted to say, ''Ugh! Oh hell!'' or whatever else I was not allowed to say.

At last I was getting in touch with the frustrations of a lifetime. It took me days to allow memories to surface, so that I could picture those who had hurt me and together with Jesus forgive them.

In the process of remembering things long forgotten, I was appalled to realize that when I taught primary grades, if anyone questioned changing a child from left to right I would assert: ''It didn't hurt me any. It made me ambidextrous. I can do anything with both hands with equal ease.'' So out of touch was I with myself!

Never did I dream the power of buried anger to imprison me for decades ''under that bushel.'' Never did I dream the power of my Bridegroom waiting from all eternity to set me free!

CHAPTER THREE

THE DESIRE OF YOUR HEART

"Franny Bride, it is your turn! What would you like your Bridegroom to do for you?" It was the summer of 1986. Our retreat team had just completed a retreat for some fifty Sisters, Brothers, and priests on God's bridal love for them. In the afterglow of the retreat, we had the habit of ministering to the parting needs of the directors.

"What would I like?" Like a hot wire I connected with a need I had ignored for months, maybe years. "The top need of my life is to know what God expects of me in the writing of my next book. I get so booked in ministry that I am afraid I could be missing God's call for writing. Ask God for me—does God want a booking of my time and when does God want it?"

Fr. Carl at once led the prayer. "Holy Spirit, show us the desire of Your heart."

"Yes, Lord, show us the desire of Your heart."

Simultaneously as we prayed in the Spirit we all agreed. In a matter of minutes, to our amazement, God made the answer ever so clear. The year to be set apart was 1988. The months were May, June, and July.

Awed by the definitiveness of the answer, I was at the same time relieved to know that May 1988 was almost two years down the pike. I would have time to "live it so that God could give it."

When I returned home to Milwaukee, there were no second thoughts or "what-ifs." Jubilantly I wiped out three months of ministry in my appointment book, my Five Year Planner. In large scrawling letters I wrote across May, June, and July of 1988—*WE, THE BRIDE*. Never had I felt so good about a booking being simultaneously booked in heaven.

Looking back over my prayer journals in the weeks, months, and years that followed, I see them sparked with words from God readying me, as bride, for a work of writing for the Bride.

I, your Bridegroom, am with you
    as the very breath that you breathe
    the thoughts that you think
    the love with which I enable you
        to reach out in love for others
            and to love yourself as I love you.

I am the LOVE within you.
    I am the PEACE within you.
    I am the still small voice that says,
        "Shhhh! Your Bridegroom is at work"
    I am the love that constantly warms,
        bathes, embraces, heals, protects,
            pours itself out upon your life.

I am in all the beauty, the riches
    the poverty that surrounds you.

I am in the choices you make
    the memories you hold of your past
        the dreams you have for your future.

I am your ALL IN ALL.
You are not alone, My Bride.
Even when you seem to be most alone and forsaken
    I, your Bridegroom, am always with you!

I believe that God is readying a Bride all over the world—people of all races, colors, creeds, denominations, masculine and feminine, rich and poor, old, young, and in-between. We are in the season of the courting of the Bride. We are in it together.

There is nothing in your life
    that is not under My total protection
    and complete care for you are My Bride.
I will care for you as the best bridegroom
in the world cares for his beloved.
    You can trust Me for this.
I am worthy of your trust.

You are right.
The Bride out there is not ready
for its Bridegroom
    nor for a book about My bridal love
    for My Bride.
But the Bride is as ready as it needs to be
    for this time of grace.
        My grace will be sufficient.
Do not be discouraged with the condition
    of the Bride.
Remember that in the Old Testament
    I took a whore for a Bride.

Ask yourself, My Bride,

"What makes you want to abandon your
  inner life for an outer life of achievement?
What causes you to get so identified
  with your work
  that you forget who you are, as Bride,
  and Who I am, as Bridegroom?"

Allow Me to be your Teacher.
It is not a simple course that you take.
It is a course that will take you a lifetime
  to learn even with Me as your Teacher.
There will never be a time when you sit back
  and say that you know it all.

Separated from Me, your Bridegroom,
  you can do nothing.
United with Me, you, the Bride,
  can truly do all things!

I want you to stay little.
When you get big I have to stand on the side
  and watch you work.
When you stay little I get to do it all.

I, the Divine Potter, have brought together
  the broken pottery that is your vessel.
I have seen it come together like the valley of
  dry bones and it is beautiful in My sight.

All the while you were ministering to others
  I was ministering to you, My Bride,
      in magnificent miracles of grace and glory.
Never fear, I am doing a sovereign work in you.
All I ask is that you move with Me in waves
  of intimacy and I will do it all.

Wonderful things are happening to you, My bride.

More and more you are checking
    for the desires of My heart before you launch
    out to undertake what you would find yourself
    doing alone.
We are truly two in one in the Father, so it is
    only right that I always be with My Bride.
It is only right that as you move throughout your day
    you can say, "WE decide, WE enjoy.
                WE serve, WE rejoice.
                WE pause to pray.
For WE are truly two in one, Bride and Bridegroom,
    in the heart of the Father."

I love you, My Bride, with a perfect love
    that cares for all the worry within you.
I do not like seeing you anxious.
In My time I will take care of all
    that is worry or anxiety within you.
You can trust your God.

I desire to give you a greater gift of prayer
    but you must earnestly desire it.
Beg for the gift and it will be yours.
This gift will lift you above the petty cares
    anxieties and contradictions of your life.
It will make it possible for all of your life
    to become prayer.

I will be there for you, My bride,
    whatever your troubles, whatever your needs.
I will be there for you, not you there for Me.
You are not there to meet My need
    but I am there to meet your every need.

When you find yourself forgetting your role as Bride
    taking on the burden of needing to change
        a loved one, a people, a church

hear the voice of your Bridegroom gently chiding:
"I am the Bridegroom; you are the Bride.
Now cool it!"

You are My fun-bride.
Never lose the spirit of fun and laughter
    for I am in it.
It is I who have given you the teaching
    on releasing the humor that was in Me
        when I walked the face of the earth.
Not only have I given you the gift to teach it
    but I have given you the gift to release it.
My bride is badly in need of
    not just a sense of humor
    but to have the very humor that was in Me
        in My humanity released in My
            very human Bride.

Tell My bride, "I gift you today
    with all the fruit of the Spirit
        that was part of My earthly life—
            My love, My joy, My peace, My patience,
            My kindness, My generosity, My humor.
All that was part of MY life
        can be part of your life."

I have used you and I will continue to use you
    to miraculously release these gifts in My Bride.

I call you to spend time in My presence
    and you will come to know Me as an intimate Lover
        ever ready to speak to you
        ever ready to give you the experience
        of being loved.
I call you to make deliberate choices to be with Me.
In times past too much of your time
        was spent separated

from the pulse of My love
    the warmth of My presence
the thoughts of My mind.
Only today you are beginning to realize how intimate
  your time with Me might have been.

When you take time to repent and ask for new grace
  there are always new beginnings.
  Today is a new beginning.
  You will never be the same again.
You have asked to be forgiven
  and I, your Bridegroom, have forgiven all.
Nothing remains except for you to say,
  "Thank You, Jesus
  for one more time forgiving your Bride."

Today began with a lot of "shoulds."
My only "should" for you is that you "should" stay
  in My presence and be moved by My Spirit
  for what you do and what you do not do.
I am the Bridegroom.
I invite, I initiate, I plan, and I arrange.
You are the Bride.
  Be encouraged to receive,
  to desire a deeper and deeper
  experience of My love.

If I have been a faithful God in the past
    a provider God in the past
    a Bridegroom God in the past
you will find Me a thousand times more in your
    todays and in your tomorrows.

For I am
  and I will be at the very core of your being
    caring for all the circumstances
      of your life.

You have married a faithful God.
The best is yet to be!
Ask for yourself and for others those graces
   and blessings that I have put close to
      your heart.
I will respond according to the measure of
   My power and My love!

Your business is to follow Me
to delight in your Bridegroom
to rejoice in what I am doing,
   not in what you are doing.
Keep your eyes on Me
   your ears tuned for My word
   your hands ready to serve Me in others
      without counting the cost.

No need for a new word when the old word is
      All that leads to intimacy, go for it!
If you follow that
   you will constantly hear My voice
   even when what I say is wordless.
Your spirit will receive the communication
     of My love.
Nothing else matters.

You will continue to grow in the gift
     of Bridal love
   and I will continue to reveal
      Myself to you
        as your Divine Bridegroom.
This is a Divine romance you are in.
All the resources of heaven and earth
   are at My disposal to court
      you as My Bride.
Be prepared for surprises!

CHAPTER FOUR

WITH GOD A DATE

"With God I have a date—In nineteen eighty-eight."

This verse was given to me as a reminder, that this was the year for that "booking" with God—May, June, and July of 1988.

Only on my January birthday did I begin to understand what God had in mind. Being a fun-bride, the idea came to me during my prayer time that day to have a truly "right-brained" birthday party. With excitement I invited the Father, Son, Holy Spirit, and the entire Heavenly Court to celebrate my birthday with praise, worship, and thanksgiving. In my faith-imagination I pictured the grand heavenly gathering in our small earthy chapel. Present were the glorious choirs of the apostles, the admirable company of the prophets, the white-robed army of martyrs, the great multitude from Revelation which no one can number, my mom, dad, godparents, all I had known and loved in this life.

Let's celebrate! How about some music?

"Give Me Your Yesterdays" was on the record player. Together with the whole heavenly court I listened to Connie Bence Boerner's song. "Give Me Your Yesterdays and let Me mend them...." Together we gave God my sixty-three years, really 23,010 yesterdays. Not only did I give them, but I trusted God to mend them. It was one gorgeous celebration of the graces, the beauty, the sunshine, the rains, the pains, the deserts, the storms, the disappointments, and the glories of all the days of my life.

When the din died down, I heard Jesus say, "All birthday parties have presents. Take your prayer journal and make a list of all your main guests. Write down what you are getting from each one. Do not debate what comes to your mind, I am as close to you as your next thought. Just write, thank, and enjoy."

The Father gave me a ring engraved, "Beloved daughter." The Holy Spirit gifted me with a new mind and a new heart cleared of all the rubbish of my past. When I got to Jesus' name, I was writing, "I am giving you a place to write *We, The Bride*."

"Wonderful," I thought, "a place to write. Right on! Thank You, Jesus!" Another round of praise and thanksgiving and the party was over.

Again I got caught up in the "in and outs" of ministry. The birthday happening was forgotten until some six weeks later, when I received a long distance call from a preferred-to-be-anonymous couple that spoke with enthusiasm: "We want to tell you this together! The Lord has been impressing upon us that we should underwrite all your expenses for your three months of writing. Will you accept the gift? You find the place and we will pay the bill."

I could hardly believe what I was hearing. "A place to write! The bill all paid. Such good news! And such a confirmation of the birthday gift that I had listed in my prayer journal weeks before! WOW!''

I was *without words!* No shopping mall in the world could hold a gift like this one! "Whoopee for God!" What else could I say?

"Whoopee for that anonymous couple!"

The rest of February, all of March, and part of April slipped by, ministry abounded—North, South, East, and West. Close to Easter I realized it was time to get my plane ticket. But for where? I had done some investigating of the possible and the desirable. Yet I had no definite sense of where God was calling me, except to a new place of trust.

In Canada after Easter, we, (Father Carl Schmidt, Frances and Dan Phillips, and myself) spent time praying and checking out with God all the possible and perhaps desirable places: Florida, Colorado, Hawaii. God cleared the board with, "None of these are My choice. I have a place in mind and if you will just be patient and trust, it will soon be revealed to you."

"Great!" With one breath I was thanking God. With the next I was panicking, "Does God know how late it is?"

Even my sleep spoke patterns of impatience. In the middle of the night I awakened, sat bolt upright in bed, and exclaimed: "How long, O Lord, how long?"

God responded, "Not long, O Fran, not long."

It wasn't long. My first night back in Milwaukee, I went to a talk on "Living the Message of Medjurgorje" given by Sister Margaret Catherine Sims from Boston. In the pre-talk time when I was visiting with Sister Margaret she asked: "Sister Fran, what are you doing now?"

"I am looking for a place to write," I popped.

Like a prophetic word coming forth at a prayer meeting Sister Margaret popped back, "I believe I have it. It is Cape Cod! There is a small cottage on the Cape right off the water. Our Sisters have spent time there. It could be a great place to write. It is spacious enough to pace. It is on a quiet street with only a five minute walk to the water. Here is the name and phone number of the lady who owns it. Phone her tomorrow to see if it is available!''

I did and it was.

To sum up the story, it was Cape Cod, a gift from God.

CHAPTER FIVE

"HERE I AM, FRAN"

In the days that followed I was in awe of God's gift as I prepared to spend three months alone with God in a place that had never entered my fondest dreams. It seemed like I was dipping into the reality of that Scripture, "Eye has not seen, nor ear heard, nor has it entered into the heart of anyone to dream what God has prepared for those who love God" (1 Cor. 2:9).

Water, yes! I dreamt of water. My dreams and longings were for a place to write with lots of water.

Trees, yes! I dreamt of trees. Some weeks before in our community prayer I had expressed my need to know something of where God was leading. In response Sister Carleen received a clear image of God's hands cupped in a thicket of trees while God's voice spoke inviting, "Here I am, Fran! Here I am!"

This image of the ever present Presence was one I

needed to keep before me both in the preparation and in the journey. "I am totally with you, not just for when you arrive at Cape Cod, but I am with you in every phase of your preparations," I recorded in my journal.

Whenever you ask Me, I am ready with a word.
I am so pleased to respond whenever I am asked.
    Surrender your burdens to Me.
It is a wedding time that we are anticipating;
    I am courting you in the now!
I send you forth with radiant hope
    born of a radiant love.
My gift to you is hope, my gift to you is love.
Whatever your problem, whatever the challenge
whatever would cause you to say, "Oh, no!"
    allow yourself to say, "Oh, yes!"
    for I am bigger than any problem, any challenge.
I am bigger than any shattered dream. Trust Me!

Wherever and whenever people prayed with me in this time of preparation there was confirmation for the job and for the journey.

Have no fear for I shall place upon your heart
    all that you need to know.
Trust Me for I shall give you
    the desire of your heart.
My nail-scarred hands shall be
    upon your hands as you write.
It is the desire of My heart for you
    to write this book.
Be totally dependent on Me and My power
    shall flow through you in abundant measure.
I shall never abandon you.

This was a totally uncharted course I was taking. No

map, no master plans, no how-to-do-it kits or manuals were available. During this time I received what Dr. Fronke and I considered a major breakthrough in my therapy. It sprang from the Scripture, "I am the Saviour of all people. Whatever their troubles I will answer their cry and I will always be their Lord" (Ps. 34:6).

I recorded the happening in my journal, "EVEN I, the Lord will be there for me. Whatever my troubles, whatever my needs, God will be there for me. Not I for God, but God for me." That could well be the hidden core of my resistance, my out-of-touchness. My core identity had been, I will be adequate for God's need. My insecurities came from the fear of not being adequate for God. The breakthrough was when I could recognize, I can need God, not just God needing me. I can be still before God, just being loved into a **new identity**, the Bride. I was readied for the journey.

May third was my take-off day for the less than two hour flight of more than a thousand miles to Boston. Sister Margaret Sims met me at the Boston airport and made the connections for my "wheels" during my stay on the Cape. As I followed Sister Margaret in the drive up Route 6A from Boston to Dennis, I sensed a whole bevy of angels traveling with us and joining us in wondrous praise and worship.

The cottage in Dennis that was to be my "holy ground" was just off Beach Road and Horsefoot Path on Coolidge Way in the elbow of the Cape, just a five minute walk from the ocean. It was late afternoon by the time we drove up to the typical Cape Cod, wooden structure with its shingled roof, a lovely framed front picture window, an old-fashioned side porch with a wooden flower box and a birdfeeder. It was painted a desert-sand yellow, to which the setting sun added a vibrant glow.

"Thank you, Father, Son, and Holy Spirit! This will be our home," with gratitude I prayed. "This will be my hermitage to spend three months alone with You. Thank

You! Thank You! Thank You!"

From within me began a churning of mixed feelings; awe, wonder, some fear, much gratitude!

Minutes before sunset we drove down to the ocean front. The sun was slowly descending. As it did, I suddenly realized that we were looking right at it. It had the appearance of a huge white host spinning off wheels of multicolored light and glory all over the slashing tidewater. "Is that like what they call the miracle of the sun in Medjugorje?" I asked Sister Margaret as we stood in awe of the indescribable beauty before us.

"It is," she said. "I have seen it many times both there and here."

For a long time we stood on the cold, white sands with a crisp, evening breeze blowing, drinking in the iridescent beauty. Through the endless rolling surf of the ocean waters God spoke:

I am so big,
    so vast, beyond your measuring or containing.
Your vision is so limited by what you see.
Your experience is so limited by what you
    sense and hear.
Allow Me to be for you, as big as the ocean
    as sure as the ocean waves.
I will be for you a voice
    when you get still enough to listen
    thirsty enough to drink
    empty enough to think new thoughts.
The new can only come from letting go of the old
    and the useless.

In that first hour of standing on the shore of the world I fell in love with the ocean, as I experienced its power to cause me to fall more and more in love with my God. I allowed it to have a mesmerizing power over me that held me in the arms of my Bridegroom God. Like a dauntless bride, I stood there allowing myself to feel loved by my Divine Lover, to feel strengthened by His strength, to feel encouraged by His courage pouring into my faltering vessel.

It was almost more than my senses could hold to know that the Father of my Bridegroom had created this vast ocean of beauty just for me. God seemed to be saying:

Here is a work of My hand
　　that you might have an inkling
　　　　of the indescribable beauty in My Godhead.
Hold it to your heart.
Treasure it.

Indescribable beauty! Unmeasurable peace! An undreamt dream come true!

I kicked up my heels in the ocean sand, whirled around and shouted for whoever would hear: "Whoopee!" To be so loved by God! From this ace of a place where lovers pace, I want to say to a world that would still doubt that it is true: "**Stop plucking daisies to find out if your God loves you**. It is true! Really, really true! GOD LOVES YOU!"

CHAPTER SIX

SHEKINAH GLORY

There was no question about this being God's chosen spot on the Cape. In the middle of the first night, as my exhausted body lay in its first sleep in the master bedroom of 15 Coolidge Way, I was awakened with the awesome awareness that the Shekinah glory was upon this place. The glow of a hundred "burning bushes" illuminated the room. Like Moses I desired to cry out: "Who are you?" But I dared not speak. I knew that I was in the presence of the great I AM.

No need to take off my shoes. I was already in my bare feet. No need to fall back under the power. I was already on my back under the power of God's holy presence. Angels from the day's journey must have filled the place with their cry: "Holy, holy, holy."

All I could do was to cry with them: "Holy, holy, holy is the Lord God of hosts. Heaven and earth are full of Your glory."

I could feel the wondrous Presence in every fiber of my being. It was a feeling of warmth like I had never known, light like I had never seen, love like I had never experienced. The presence of the Almighty was penetrating every facet of my existence—past, present, and future.

For a long time I remained immobile with my eyes closed, knowing that the glory of the Lord was upon me. Bathed in this glory, I was afraid to open my eyes for fear that if I did, I would see God there. I didn't feel that I was ready for that.

There was nothing I could do but to allow the darkness of a thousand nights to be illumined in the light of this night, to listen for the wordless promise of the Bridegroom that He would not forsake me, to be assured that We, The Bride would come to birth in this place. My stilled body spoke the wordless fiat—be it done according to Your promise.

Early the next morning I was awakened to begin my first day on the Cape, with the glow and the glory still heavy upon me. I was too energized to sleep. Before the sun was up, I was up taking an extended time of worship and praise to declare this cottage a dwelling place for the Almighty, the King of kings, the Bridegroom of my soul.

With Integrity's tape on my recorder, I was able to fill the place with a fully orchestrated version of the exalted strains of "We are standing on holy ground and I know that there are angels all around...."

I knew that there were angels all around. They were with me on yesterday's journey flying the "Friendly Skies" to Boston, and encircling my 1970 station wagon cruising along highway 6A to Dennis. Angels were part of last night's round of glory. Today I could join in their chorus of worship and praise as I declared 15 Coolidge Way Holy Ground for praying and for waiting.

I was particularly aware of the presence of my two guardian angels; Amen and Hallelujah. These are names that I was given years ago for them. It had been confirmed

to me several times when I was teaching or ministering
that someone saw two angels ministering with me. I made
certain that they were welcomed and honored in this
place where I would be alone with God for three months.
With ceremony I placed my two Fra Angelico angel icons
on the cottage wall of the front room that was to become
my prayer room. As I did a childhood prayer sprang to
my lips:

> Angel of God, my guardian dear
> To whom God's love commits me here.
> Ever this day be at my side
> To light and guide, to rule and guide.

The sun was still below the horizon and I was ready
for my first full-blown prayer time on the Cape. Desiring
to be led by the Spirit I prayed: "Holy Spirit, what is the
desire of Your heart?"

With the swiftness of my next thought the answer
came: "Enthrone your Bible. Enter into praise and thanksgiving for the presence of the Word. Ask for a word."

From my well-packed luggage I brought forth the
cherished Book, a large, deerskin-covered *New American
Bible*. I had received this treasure from Father John Hascal
when I was ministering in his Native-American parish.
With a special prayer for the Native-American Bride I
exuberantly held God's Word on high, knowing that it was
full of living power for me. Indeed it was sharper than the
sharpest sword to do battle for me, and to cut deep into
my innermost thoughts and desires revealing both the
Bridegroom and the Bride.

As I enthroned the Word, I knew that I could boldly
approach the very throne of God with confidence. And as
the Word from Hebrews affirms, I knew that I could stay in
the throne room to receive mercy, favor, and help in time
of need. I had a Bridegroom, High Priest, who could
sympathize with my every weakness. I did not need to be

adequate for God. God would be adequate for me.

Outside a liquid glow of early morning sun was just beginning to blazon the sky. A stream of it poured through my picture window. As it did I allowed its energy and warmth to embrace me while I prayed: "Jesus, please give Your bride a special word for this first day; something You would like me to think and to pray about as I enter with You into this courting season."

"Who is this coming up from the desert, like a column of smoke, laden with myrrh, with frankincense, and with perfume of every exotic dust?" With awe I realized that I had opened to the Song of Songs 3:6.

In the footnotes I read: "My Beloved was coming in royal procession to meet His Bride."

With the swiftness of a gazelle, a part of me wanted to leap forth to meet my Beloved. Another part with equal swiftness wanted to evaporate into one of those miniscule desert sands. For who am I to be called here by the Almighty, to receive not just a word but a whole book of words for the Bride of such a regal Bridegroom?

Who am I to be coming up from my desert with nothing of greatness in my roots, or my sands?

Who am I but a farm girl from Iowa, a charismatic nun of 20 years vintage, School Sister of Notre Dame of 43 years maturing? Who am I to gather together an experimental expose of what I see happening to the Bride?

Who am I to receive not a new revelation but a revelation of the Revelation of who the Bridegroom is for the Bride and who the Bride is for the Bridegroom?

Who am I to be anticipating the God of Abraham, the God of Moses, of Isaiah, of Judith, of Ruth, of Esther, the God of Zechariah, of Elizabeth, of John the Baptist, of Mary to speak a word to me for *We, The Bride*?

Who am I to be hoping for the Lord God Almighty, the Lion of the tribe of Judah, the Ruah of the Old Testament, to meet me in my twentieth century desert?

In the flesh there was no way to answer any of these

questions. In the Spirit there was a way to answer all of them. In an extended time of worship, I gave voice to both questions and answers in my prayer language.

If ever I sensed the illimitable value of tongues (or as I have come to call it, a Father, Son, and Holy Spirit language), I experienced it that morning and everyday throughout my stay. With infinite variety I could yield myself to praying and to singing in the Spirit whenever there was no "left-brained" way to comprehend either the call or the move of God.

As I took to praying in my prayer language, in one "quantum leap" I was into the heart of my Abba and my Emma, into the arms of my Bridegroom, and into the consuming love and fire of the Holy Spirit. In that Heart, in those Arms, in that Fire, I knew that not only was I asking the right questions but I knew that I was receiving the right answers.

With the sounds of many tongues I prayed for the people of many nations, the Bride of many nations. In the Spirit I was receiving, answering, worshiping for the Bride that was European, Asian, African, Australian, South American and American. The answer was not simple. It was profoundly full of mystery, wonder, beyond thought, beyond words.

I have heard tongues described as "voiced contemplation," or a prayer not unlike infused contemplation, because in both the mind is unfruitful. I desired very much to understand my call to write and the forms it would take. However, from the beginning I realized that this was not to be my gift, for my mind was unfruitful, while my spirit was abounding in the fruit of the Spirit. I was being filled with peace, joy, patience, long-suffering...and all the rest of those good Galatian fruit that cannot be bought at the supermarket.

Who is this coming up from the desert? Together with the Bridegroom, I could envision the Bride, national and international, denominational and interdenominational, active and contemplative, yuppie and third-world. I could see a beautiful Bride alive in the Spirit walking with Jesus. In the Spirit I could hear: ''How beautiful you are, My love, how beautiful you are!'' (Song of Songs 4:1).

I looked at my watch. It was less than twenty-four hours since I left behind the world I knew in Milwaukee. For a moment there was a twinge of loneliness. ''I am all alone here on the Cape!''

''Alone? Come, My promised Bride, and inhabit this place. Live in this place and you will know My Presence!''

No more shall people call you "Forsaken,"
   or your land "Desolate,"
But you shall be called "My Delight,"
   and your land "Espoused."
For the Lord delights in you,
   and makes your land His spouse.
As a young man marries a virgin,
   your Builder shall marry you;
And as a bridegroom rejoices in his bride
   so shall your God rejoice in you.
               (Isa. 62:4-5).

CHAPTER SEVEN

THE PRESENT OF GOD'S PRESENCE

The awareness of God's presence was a constant gift for my three month stay on the Cape. When I realized that I had the same amount of time that Mary had spent with Elizabeth and Zechariah in the hill country of Judah, these words from Luke 1:45-47 took on special meaning for me: "Blest is she who trusted that the Lord's words to her would be fulfilled." Then Mary said: "My being proclaims the greatness of the Lord, and my spirit finds joy in God, my Saviour."

Unlike the hill country of Judah, Dennis, Massachusetts was more of a plain carpeted with trees, holly, scrub pine, silver maple, locust, and oak, with an occasional elevated area to view the rest of the scenic coast. This was a season when almost every home and roadside was alive with the yellow bell-shaped forsythia, blooms which appear in the early spring before the leaves sprout out.

"The winter is past, the rains are over and gone. The flowers appear on the earth" (Song of Songs 2:11-12). These words became my theme song during those first weeks of being courted by God. It seemed that every flowering bush, tulip, and daffodil bore a tag for me: "With love from your God." On the beaches in the sand dunes the purple and white beach peas, the shadbush, the yellow hudsomia all made their spring debut in keeping with the promise of the canticle, "The flowers appear on the earth."

Though my call was for a time of solitude with my Bridegroom, I was pleased to be encouraged to enjoy deviations like attending daily Mass and the Wednesday night prayer meeting at a cozy community church, Our Lady of the Cape. To arrive there was a nine mile nature jaunt, in and out of wooded back roads connecting with the main highway. This small but powerful group of Capers were my booster cable when my battery ran low. They were my God "with skin on" in times when solitude became overwhelming. They were a live symbol of the Bride I was being called to write for.

During one of my first cottage prayer times I received the invitation to come into the desert of His heart. I asked Jesus why He called it a desert. He said:

Because there is nothing there but Me.
There is nothing there but My presence.
There is nothing flowering except My love.
If you are looking for something else
    it is not there.

If you are thirsting for union with Me
    you will find it in the desert of My heart.
There is nothing but Me to love
    nothing but Me to see
    nothing but Me to hear
    nothing but Me to experience.

Come My Bride, into the desert of My heart
    for I see in your heart a thirst
    for a deeper experience of your Bridegroom.
You will have it.
It will be a desert experience.
You will come to love the desert.
You will come to know that each step on the
    burning sand is a step closer to Me.

I will never leave you alone
    to wander in the desert.
I will always be there to walk with you
    hand in hand,
    heart in heart,
    thought in thought.
I will be there to feed you
        on the Living Word.
I will be there to quicken
        your ears to My voice
In the desert of stillness.

In the desert is freedom from distractions.
It is easy there to keep your eyes on Me
    for I am all there is.
You will find Me
    in the very center of your being.
I am the Lord of the desert.
I am in control.
You do not need to control the desert.
You do not need to plan your desert experience.
It is all planned.

Early May on the Cape is totally out of season for
tourists. It was a great season for me to be an anchorite.
Layered in my Irish knit and purple windbreaker, I spent
hours of quiet contemplation and active prayer, gleefully

treading the ocean sands. Sometimes I would find a snug little desert corner where I could sit to drink in the bigness of God to the tune of the slashing water, my own heart, and the added tunes of worship and praise from my cassette recorder.

Just one sentence from Scripture like: "The hungry, God has filled with good things" (Luke 1:53), would occupy me for hours. In my spirit I got in touch with all the hungers of the Bride across the world: the physical hungers, the psyche hungers, and the spiritual hungers. In one grand swoop of prayer I would lift the hungry to the heavens. I would pray in tongues in any one of twenty-four hundred languages of the world, in sounds and syllables that came from the Spirit. As I prayed I could picture the feast, earthly and heavenly, that was being spread for a hungry world, for a hungry Bride whose greatest hunger is to know the living God.

In the words of Mary in her hill-country canticle, I would proclaim for the whipping waves to hear: "God has filled the hungry with good things and the rich, God has turned away empty."

"His mercy is from age to age." In my prayer language I would cry out for mercy. I would plead God's marvelous mercy for all the ways the universal Bride is resisting, denying, prostituting the love of the Divine Bridegroom. In my spirit I could see huge tidal waves of mercy going forth, mercy for the poor, the destroyed, the homeless; mercy for the sick, the addicted, the afflicted; mercy for those filled with power, prestige, and possessions but empty and without peace.

The more I cried out for Divine Mercy the more I knew that mercy is a key gift for the twentieth century Bride of Jesus. Mercy means we do not deserve a thing. All is gift. Our Bridegroom simply gifts us and loves us in all our imperfections, incompleteness, and sinfulness because He is Love in all its fullness. In His sweet mercy Jesus embraces us just as we are, with a love that is unmerited, unconditional, and unlimited.

There were times when I could sense a Divine typewriter going back and forth with words for *We, The Bride*, while my very limited being was proclaiming to the water and the waves the magnitude of my God: "God who is mighty has done great things. Holy is God's name."

"Sing a new song unto the Lord!" I must have sung a thousand new songs unto the Lord on the shores of Cape Cod—songs that no one had ever sung. There on the ocean sands I was given both the words and the melodies to sing them in the Spirit.

"There are many songs in My Father's heart that no one has ever sung," Jesus said to me one day, "and I am going to give you one." In reality He gave me many new songs. Sometimes I would get new words for old melodies like: "I am the Bridegroom and you are the Bride. The banner over us is love. You are My joy, My dance, and My song. The banner over us is love." The chorus for "Our God Reigns" became, "I'm in love, I'm in love, I'm in love with my God." There were no boring moments in this courting season, for I never knew when Jesus would sing a love song to me through my own lips. One night I was awakened with this tune orchestrating through me with full organ accompaniment:

> Here comes the bride
> All beautiful inside
> Oh how I love
> My beautiful, beautiful bride.

I just knew that it was not up to me to limit the ways in which my Bridegroom would choose to manifest himself. More and more I came to know that the real world is the world of the unseen much more than the world of the seen, and that I could trust my spiritual being to communicate the reality. To be so aware of God's presence truly could have been a grace given because of all the prayers prayed for me by the Bride around the world.

Father, Son, and Holy Spirit bless and guide
Sister Fran in her writing of *We, The Bride*.

In 1987 I was given this prayer verse to encourage people from across the world to pray for the success and the right timing in my writing. I am grateful for their part in the birthing of this book.

Knowing myself and my Meyers-Briggs personality type, without prayer support I could have been stalemated in my solitude in one magnificent web of loneliness. On the contrary these three months were high adventure for me. To see how my Bridegroom would choose to reveal himself with a word, an image, a Scripture, a song at the most unlikely times, and places was HIGH ADVENTURE!

"Hark! My lover! Here He comes springing across the mountains, leaping across the hills. My lover is like a gazelle or a young stag. He looks in at a window. He peers through the lattice" (Song of Songs 2:8-9).

A love affair with God is rich in intrigue. There was hardly a roadway or path where I did not feel hugged by an abundance of trees with their budding branches arching over the highways. "Here I am, Fran," they seemed to say in keeping with Carleen's vision. Several times I was impelled to stop my car to immortalize a picture of what I saw: My Bridegroom's hands cupped in a thicket of silver maples calling out, "Here I am, Fran!"

To my delightful surprise, God was not only in the forsythia, the ocean surf, the thickets of trees, the limited folk I chose to know, but I discovered God the day of my first mail-pickup behind the wall of my mail box. This is the letter I found with the outside addressed, "Franny, the Bride."

Dear Fran,

I had wanted to see you before you left, to give you a hug and to wish you well, as you draw apart to write as "Bride." The hug means and represents different things to me. I wanted to hug you in encouragement! A hug that says: I love you, I support you, my heart carries you, and I lift you to the heavens in prayer. I take you to the Father, best I can.

I hug you in the spirit of truth, on behalf of the "faithful" that say I am broken and needy. I am both sinner and redeemed. And sometimes I don't know which to believe is my center. I am afraid and childlike in my heart. I live in a grown-up world that does not accept the trusting child-of-God in me.

Perhaps more simply, I seek the peace that surpasses understanding within, while the world I live in is harsh, glaring, threatening, and I am invaded by it all. So can you convince me that Jesus really does love me? He really wants to call me bride? How do I dare risk enough to allow Jesus, the Bridegroom, into my heart? How do I abandon myself to Him? How do I make it safe enough to try?

You might say that to call me (us) Bride, you are trying to put the finest robe and crown of jewels on a garbage dump. That's how I feel (when you get down into the heart and conscience of me). Or something to that effect.

My head, my intellectual process, could argue against this and with some truth, but my guts say that I am guilty. I am really not O.K. I don't measure up and that kind of stuff.

And I *want to be one with Jesus*, the Lord!
Yes, Wow!

Finally I hug you on behalf of Him, the Groom. ''My hug is both a proposal and an invitation to draw apart, to be one, to be shown love, the depths of it. It is an invitation to laugh and cry together, to embrace and play together, to be renewed and refreshed, in the presence of each other. Finally and lastly I invite you to be a 'voice' to My people.''

Dear Franny of God, I will continue to love you and to pray for you through the entire season of your engagement. I do not expect you to answer my letters. That is not your assignment. But I will continue to drop you a line, now and then. Just a word from the streets, as it were, because I think this is one tough assignment!

Peace and blessings abundant to you! I am with you—best I can. I love you—best I can. God bless you, Fran!

In His Name, Shalom!

Ken

Ken is a recovering alcoholic who discovered Jesus, the Bridegroom, at one of our retreats.

CHAPTER EIGHT

GARBAGE MAN JESUS

Months before my journey, God gave this word to me through Sister Mary,

You are about to begin a new journey.
I am drawing you into the desert of My heart.
There I will speak My words to you.
The fire of My Spirit will be upon you.
I will speak the words that
        I want My people to hear.
I have called you and I will not fail you.
I will be with you on this journey.

What God did not say until a few days after I arrived at the Cape was:

I have even provided for you a little desert

right outside this cottage
>   that you might dwell more graphically
>   in the desert of My heart.
You had so hoped and dreamed of a cottage
>   lush with New England flowers, foliage, and grass.
But for My own purposes I have allowed
>   the desert sands to surround your cottage
>   instead of all that could have been
>   most scenic and lovely.

"God! I am really disappointed, not in You, but in the circumstances. You are right, my dreams and visions were for a place lush with flowers and greenery of all sorts. After living for seven years above a school with no front or back yard, I was anticipating greenery and flowers of all sorts that I could call my own—lovely New England salt-spray roses, blueberry bushes, tulips, daffodils, irises, hydrangeas, and azaleas!"

By now I knew the circumstance. My landlady had shared that in the preceding year this cottage had needed a new foundation. All the usual exterior Cape Cod beauty was sacrificed in the rebuilding of the foundation. Nothing remained of the former beauty. There were no bushes, no foliage, no perennials, no grass. There were only the desert sands and yellow dandelions!

A few days after saying: "It's okay God to have just desert sands and yellow dandelions!" I became acutely aware that I was being called to be content with not just what was missing, but with what was left littering up my back yard. As neighbor after neighbor began "sprucing up" for the new season, I realized that my back yard was greatly in need of a massive clean-up and clear-out. It looked like there was no one but me to move a devastating pile-up of brambles, broken branches, a smashed-down picnic table, and ugly rusted broken pipes! Quite simply there was no one but me to clear away an unbelievable heap of back yard rubbish.

This was a real eyesore for someone with a system geared to: "If you're going to throw something away, do it today, not tomorrow, not next week or next month. Do it today!" As I looked out of my window I could feel my blood pressure rise. A core of buried anger began to escalate and I blurted out for whomever to hear: "Why can't that landlady get rid of that rubbish?"

From therapy I remembered that my need is to stand in my authentic self and express my feelings, perception, and need. I spoke it out, gut to mouth: "I feel angry. It seems to me that I am being subjected to a heap of rubbish that belongs to someone else. Landlady, I need you not to subject me to a heap of someone else's rubbish!"

If only to the four walls, I said it! A feeling of contentment began to rise in me.

I had almost forgotten that Jesus is the silent Listener to every conversation or solo speech until I heard the voice of my Bridegroom say: "Why don't you use it as a symbol, a visual for your life? This courting season is for a clearing out of all the useless, broken-down, outdated clutter, junkitis, rubbish of your inner life. Franny, My bride, did I hear you say yes to a massive inner-being clean up job?"

"Yes, Jesus, yes!" This was a moment of grace. I continued: "As You were the eternal YES to the Father, I desire to be an eternal yes to You. Whatever must go, must go! I say yes to You, Father! Yes to You, Jesus! Yes to You, Holy Spirit! Yes to a massive inner clean-up job of my life!

"Father, You are the Vinedresser, root up everything in me that You did not plant. Jesus, You are the Temple Cleaner, cleanse my Temple of all that blocks our bridal relationship, all that keeps me from thinking bridal thoughts, feeling bridal feelings, moving in bridal ways. Holy Spirit, of wind, of fire, of power, come like a mighty bulldozer to clear out all that no longer fits the life of a Bride of the King of kings and Lord of lords! Father, Son, and Holy Spirit, I give You permission to do an ongoing massive clean-up job of my life."

In the heavens there echoed a thunderous, "Amen!"

This was followed by a praying spree in my prayer language, so that the Holy Spirit could say for me all the things that needed to be said but which I had no concept or word to express with my natural mind. By then I was so enthused about the back yard imagery for my inner being that I got my Fuji camera and took several pictures of the now memorable back yard rubbish.

I was about to conclude my prayer when I sensed Jesus winking and saying:

No bill from the garbage collector!
And tell My Bride out there
    no matter how much rubbish or sin
        needs to be cleared out of their lives
with God all things are possible!
No pile-up is too high or too great!
No rubbish is immovable or hopeless!
No need to have front yards, back yards,
    real lives stashed away with unviewable
        debris, devastating sin!
Whatever your condition, whatever your rubbish
    your Bridegroom says:
        "I am the garbage collector.
        Got any garbage I can take out?"

CHAPTER NINE

I WILL LEAD YOU INTO THE DESERT

My need was great. I needed to enter into the deep mysteries and infinite treasures of bridal love, to discover its eternal secrets, to be disciplined in the art of constantly yielding to God's purpose, plan, and timing. God's assurance came once again, ''I will be adequate for you. You do not need to be adequate for Me.''

God was not distant. God was as close as my next thought. Throughout my stay I was blessed to have a recorder to capture some of the flow of thoughts that punctuated each day.

An article I read some years ago in a magazine on ''How to pray always'' helped me to do just that—to pray without ceasing. In this article the author asked, how can we do what Paul says: ''Pray without ceasing'' (1 Thess. 5:17). By way of answer another question was raised. What is something we always do? Talk? No! Think? Yes! So if you can make of your thoughts a dialogue rather than a monologue you would be praying always.

For years I have been working to make it work. It has worked for me. Sometimes it has worked with a bit of humor such as: "Oh God, I didn't think that. Honest I didn't."

I would hear: "Oh yes, you did, and it wasn't nice! So here's a better thought right out of My mind." I would let go of my thought for God's thought. This can be a mind stretching but rewarding way to live as Bride.

To nourish bridal love for Jesus, we need to be intimate, to enjoy His indwelling, to anticipate His speaking at any time, in any place, in any circumstance.

"Speak Lord, Your servant is listening" is one of my favorite one-liner prayers. One day Jesus beat me to it with: "Speak Fran, your God is listening."

I spoke, and then Jesus spoke:

Even as the Spirit led Me into the desert
for forty days to fast and pray
to ready Myself for My public ministry
so the Spirit is calling you, the Bride,
into the desert that you may fast and pray
     and be readied for the ministry
          God is calling you to.

As you fast and pray unite yourself with
     My prayer and fasting in the desert.
Since we are two in one,
     your prayer and your fasting
     will take on the power
     of My prayer and My fasting
          before the throne of My Father.

Fear not, beloved Bride,
     to come up from your desert
     leaning on the arm of Jesus,

your Bridegroom, into the very
   presence of your Heavenly Father.
Fear not to find your place to worship and
   to rest in the Heavenly Throne room.
You are invited to join in the praise and worship
   of the Bride triumphant,
     the apostles, martyrs, prophets, patriarchs
     the saints who have gone before you.

I have given you a prayer language
   that you might have words to worship
     in the many tongues
     of many peoples of all times.
I constantly give to you new songs
   that you might blend your song with the
     worshiping multitudes in the heavenlies.

"Alleluia! Salvation, glory and might belong to our God. Let us rejoice and be glad, and give God glory! For this is the wedding day of the Lamb, His bride has prepared herself for the wedding. She has been given a dress to wear made of finest linen, brilliant white. Happy are they who have been invited to the wedding feast of the Lamb" (Rev. 19:1, 5-9).

You, My Bride
   are invited to the
     Wedding Feast of the Lamb.
Indeed the desert will be for you
   a place to prepare and to long for
     the real Wedding Feast of the Lamb.
It will be a place where what is earthy
   can be lifted to the heavens
   and what is heavenly
     can be visited upon the earth.
I will be with you in every phase
   of the celebration.

I will be the song on your lips
   the fire in your heart
   the light for your path.
I will not leave you alone
   to your whims and fancies.
Ask and I will give you clear direction
   for every step of the journey.

Bride of the Lamb,
I will take you more deeply into the desert
   than I have in the past.
As I do, I am creating within you a new hunger
   and a new thirst to love and to be loved.

I am creating a hunger to know the love
   of your Father, as I know that love.
I am creating a hunger to know the love
   of your Bridegroom Who is love.
I am creating a thirst to be filled with
   the Living Water
      that is the Spirit of Love.
We are creating in you, beloved Bride,
   a new emptiness and a new brokenness
      that We may fill the emptiness
     with Our incredible riches
     and heal the brokenness with
       Our illimitable power.

This is not something you can do.
It is something We do for the Bride
   when the Bride says, ''yes'' to the desert.
It is a sovereign work.
It is Our power to match your need.

   ''The Bridegroom is waiting to show you favor and
rises to pity you for your Bridegroom is a God of justice.
Happy are all who wait for Him! He will be gracious to

you when you cry out; as soon as He hears He will answer you. No longer will your Bridegroom hide Himself, but with your own eyes you shall see Him'' (Isa. 30:18-21; my paraphrase).

Deserts are not just for a day but for a season. Moses, Isaiah, Jeremiah, John the Baptist, Jesus had their seasons in the deserts. My season from the beginning was permeated with the Isaiah promise that my desert would bloom. ''The desert and the parched land will exult: the steppe will rejoice and bloom. They will bloom with abundant flowers, and rejoice with joyful song. The glory of Lebanon will be given to them, the splendor of Carmel and Sharon: They will see the glory of the Lord, the splendor of our God'' (Isa. 35:1-2).

The Lord encouraged and boosted my belief that my desert would bloom. On one of my first trips to the Purity Supreme Supermarket, I was urged by the Lord to stop by a roadside floral shop to buy a gorgeous full-flowered New Guinea impatiens plant to hang in my picture window. It was to be a symbol of the promise that my desert would bloom.

''Twenty-two dollars and five cents! Are You sure that I should be buying a plant at that price?'' I debated within myself.

''It is a gift from your Bridegroom! I have already supplied the means.'' In the mail that day I had received a twenty-five dollar check marked for a special gift.

All through the aisles of the supermarket and for the rest of the day as I made choices I would hear, ''It is a gift from your Bridegroom!'' While I was stacking my groceries on the checkout counter, I was very much aware that all is gift to be reverenced and thanked for.

This same thought is beautifully expressed in our SSND Constitution, YAS (You Are Sent): ''We regard all as gift and ourselves as stewards of whatever is entrusted to us.'' (YAS, p. 26) A cottage at Cape Cod for three months was far from the usual for gift or for stewardship for an

SSND. I was in awe of the privilege of having Cape Cod as an extension of my official assignment, Charismatic Spiritual Renewal Travel Ministry.

In keeping with my life as an SSND, daily I would renew my vows with a prayer like: "Jesus, my Bridegroom, I am Yours forever without reserve in gospel poverty." One day as I paused Jesus continued: "Franny, My bride, I am yours forever without reserve in gospel riches."

Stripped of everything but the basics my desert spot was a splendid place to learn what gospel riches are. In the unfolding beauty of creation I discovered some of these riches. As I paced the Mayflower beach, watched the tides come in and out, and stilled my being before the extravagances of an ocean sunrise and sunset, I knew that I was "the richest kid on the block."

Day by day, I discovered riches in the deepest core of my being. I studied the Word and delighted anew in the pages of YAS, "We come to the Father through Jesus in the power of the Spirit. From Jesus, our Bridegroom we learn what it means to be in union with and sent by the Father" (YAS, p. 30).

The call to union and the mission of being sent was confirmed over and over in the Scriptures and in the words of YAS I knew the sustaining grace of being sent by Jesus and the Father to do this writing.

Because this was a "desert" place, it was not unusual for me in my prayers to be shifting from moments of glory to desperation: "Oh God, what am I doing here? What in heaven's name is the purpose of all this prayer, of all this waiting on You for a message for the Bride?"

There were days when I felt like a Moses in the desert, a Daniel in the lion's den, a John on Patmos!

"God, what am I doing here?" I would cry out.

God's answer came in many ways. One day it was in a statement from YAS, pages 30 and 31: "Slowly, irresistibly, our Bridegroom draws us more deeply into Himself, transforming us into the Divine Image....In prayer we acknowledge, accept, and freely surrender to the reality of who God is and who we are, creatures unconditionally loved by our Bridegroom.''

There was no resistance to the drawing, no resistance to the transforming. There was only a greater and greater desire to be surrendered to the transforming power, and a greater and greater desire to be surrendered to the bliss of His bridal love. My desire was to hear Him say in the words of Hosea: ''I will betroth you to Me forever; I will betroth you to Me in righteousness and in justice, in steadfast love, and in mercy. I will betroth you to Me in faithfulness; And you shall know the Lord'' (Hos. 2:19-20).

One of the marks of Bridehood on Steve Fry's tapes on *The Coming Revelation of the Bride* is to be constantly asking the question, ''Lord, what would glorify You the most?''

For years this question had been in the foreground for me, guiding the decisions of my daily living, ''Holy Spirit, what is the desire of Your heart?''

The answer often led me to let go of things that really were not important, in lieu of what was important in living out my bridal relationship with Jesus. Whatever leads to intimacy—**Go for it!** Whatever doesn't—**who needs it**? This was a definite help in tailoring the kind of TV shows I might choose to watch. Also as I went shopping in the mall I was aware of needing to ask the question before settling on a purchase—''Holy Spirit, is it the desire of Your heart that I buy this?''

Sometimes in bigger things I have found it helpful to check to see if I am hearing right for the desires of God's heart. I am remembering the day that I asked a friend to check out the Lord's call on my life to write and to pray for a special anointing for that call. The prophetic answer came:

Have no fear!
For I shall place upon your heart
   all that you need to know.
I say to you, My daughter, trust Me.
Trust Me for I shall give you
   the desires of your heart.

You shall know that you are inspired
   of Me to write this book.
It will not only be divinely guided
   but it will be inspired.
I shall enlighten your mind as you write.

I want you to surrender yourself
   entirely to Me.
There are times when you are concerned and
   deeply troubled about where to go
      and what to do.
I want you to surrender yourself totally
   to Me, to be totally dependent upon
      Me and upon My power.

My power shall flow through you in greater
   measure as you depend totally on Me.
You shall know that it is I
   Who am using you in a powerful way
      to set My people free from the bondage
      of not knowing Me as the Lord of their
      lives and the Bridegroom of their souls.

At times you have difficulty sensing
   peace in your heart.
You are restless and unsure
   that the work I call you to do will be
   done as I would have you do it.
In those times I want you to reflect
   on My Passion and the love that

I have for My beloved Bride.

As you do you will receive greater
    wisdom in writing for I shall
        never abandon you.
I shall be with you always,
    as close as your next thought
    prompting you, inspiring you,
    loving you as My own child
        a Bride created in My own image
    to fellowship with Me and My Bride
        for all eternity.

These words spoke courage and hope for me in my solitude spot. To see God's words black on white affirmed me especially in times when I could be plagued with doubts and second thoughts. They were a launching pad to praise my Bridegroom for the gift of anointed and dedicated friends. They also led me into a time of repentance for all the ways I had rebelled against and resisted the call to write again. In the Spirit I could see my skid marks all over the "King's Highway," the no, the yes, the maybe, the sometime, all in pure contrast to the way Mary responded in her Magnificat, "be it done to me according to Your Word."

In those early days I did a lot of begging for the grace of faithfulness to God's call and God's timing. With the gift of "tongues" I prayed a lot for the gift of "ears."

CHAPTER TEN

POWER FOR THE COURSE

Speak Lord, your Bride is listening. Is there anything You want to say to your Bride today? Often I would begin the day's routine with this prayer question, but not until I had done my daily three.

Number One—Daily making Jesus the Lord of my life. Using the Scripture: "If I be lifted up, I will draw all people unto Me" (John 12:32). I would lift up Jesus, as the Lord of my life and the Bridegroom of my soul. With crucifix in hand, I would proclaim Jesus Lord of all the adventures, the circumstances, the challenges, and the difficulties of that day.

Each day the proclamation was different and unique. Often I could blend it with tongues, knowing that when the Bridegroom comes in the great Parousia, every knee shall bow, every tongue confess that Jesus Christ is Lord. In my prayer languages I would proclaim in ways I never could in English, that Jesus Christ is Lord! Lord of my life! Lord of my family, my community, my church! Lord of this day! Lord of this writing! I am the instrument. Jesus is the Lord!

Truly this prayer established me in peace for whatever the day would bring. Jesus was the Lord of this courting season. My bridal walk was under His Lordship. I could look to Him to ''call the shots.'' As His Bride I could relax and enjoy every ecstatic and beautiful moment! Daily I found real joy in proclaiming the Lordship of Jesus in song:

> Lord, You are more precious than silver.
> Lord, You are more costly than gold.
> Lord, You are more beautiful than diamonds.
> And nothing I desire compares with You.
>
> Lynn deShazo

> For You are Lord! You are Lord!
> You are risen from the dead and You are Lord!
> Every knee shall bow! Every tongue confess
> that Jesus Christ is Lord!
>
> Author unknown

Basking daily in the truth of the Lordship of Jesus deepened the assurance that I was indeed a princess, a bride of the Risen King and that I was destined for the throne. ''Fear not, for it is your Father's good pleasure to give you the Kingdom'' (Luke 12:32). ''Those who prove victorious I will allow to share My throne just as I was victorious Myself and took My place with My Father on His throne'' (Rev. 3:21).

The key to victorious living was not just the daily proclamation of the Lordship of Jesus but **Number Two**—taking authority over everything that would block His Lordship. For this I used this prayer.

PRAYER TO TAKE AUTHORITY

"In the Name of Jesus, I take authority and I bind all powers and forces in the air, in the ground, in the water, in the underground, in the nether world, in nature, and in fire.

"You are the Lord over the entire universe and I give You the glory for Your creation. In Your name I bind all demonic forces that have come against us and our families and I seal all of us in the protection of Your Precious Blood that was shed for us on the Cross....

"Michael and our guardian angels come and defend us and our families in battle against all the evil ones that roam the earth.

"In the name of Jesus I bind and command all the powers and forces of evil to depart right now away from us, our homes and our lands. And I thank you Lord Jesus for You are a faithful and compassionate God. Amen."

I know of no prayer more necessary nor more effective in blocking the powers of darkness than this "Prayer to Take Authority." It needs to be said with authority or it is meaningless. When said with authority power it can be "power for the course!"

Number Three—was to ask Jesus to baptize me anew in the Holy Spirit each day. Depending on how I was feeling, I would ask for a new fullness of the Holy Spirit to fit my needs for that day. There were days when I felt the need for a baptism of love. On other days it was for the baptism of peace, of truth, of joy, of wisdom, of understanding, of energy.

My belief is that you get what you pray for. I believe that each day I experienced a new immersion in the fullness of the Holy Spirit Who is the fullness of Light, Life, and Love—a fullness of Light to cast out all darkness—a fullness of Life to renew my life—a fullness of Love to flood my heart with bridal love for Jesus! That is power for the course!

Daily I pray in my prayer language for at least one-half hour often with taped music playing, asking for an increase and release of all the gifts, all the power, and all the fruit of the Holy Spirit.

I pray for the **Inspirational gifts**:
1. Gift of Faith Believer's and Expectant
2. Word of Wisdom
3. Word of Understanding

The **Word gifts**
4. Tongues and Interpretation of Tongues
   Diversified Tongues
5. Word of Knowledge
6. Prophecy and Prophetic Word

The **Miracle gifts**
7. Healing Prayer and Healing Love
   Surge of Healing Power
   Miraculous Power
8. Miraculous healing
9. Deliverance
   Inner healing
   Casting out spirits
10. Visions, signs, and wonders
11. Discerning of spirits
12. Discernment of God

Remember: We get it the way we pray for it!

I have shared with you my daily three for if there is one common prophecy heard all over the world it is: "Power will not be lacking to you for the work God is calling you to do." On the other hand if there is one common condition that I have heard from the Bride all over the world it is: "We need power! We are dragging!

The attacks of the enemy are so strong!"

We are a perfect fit for Hebrews 12:12-13: "So strengthen your drooping hands and your weak knees. Make straight the paths you walk on, that your halting limbs may not be dislocated but healed."

The Daily Three is power! It is strength for "your drooping hands and your weak knees!" It was strength for mine as each day I could leave my bedroom singing: "The Spirit of the Lord is upon me and He has anointed me, His bride, to do great things today in power!"

If you want to know the secret that empowered me day by day to move from prayer time to prayer time, I have just shared it with you. My daily one, two, three set the stage for whatever else the Lord would have me do to become the bearer of His Word.

Tell My Bride that
You have never been so beautiful to behold
                    so charming to court
                    so precious to love!
I have never been more in love with you!
I have never been more eager for your
                    return of love!

This is the season for the courting of the Bride.
You, My beautiful, chosen people are the Bride
        that I am courting from the heights
                of the heavens
        from the pulpits of your churches
        the valleys and the mountain tops
                of your retreats
        the speakers' stands of your conferences
        the spaces of your prayer closets.

Today I invite each of you to say yes
            to My courting you
        to say yes to My wooing you

yes to My loving you.
Do not resist My bridal love!
Do not debate it, weigh it,
    or try to comprehend it!
Simply receive it as pure gift
    from the heart of your God.
It is one of those surprises of the Holy Spirit
    that no one dreamed possible or desirable
    but **it is for today**.
It is for all of My people
    who will say yes to it.

Never have I been more ready
    to gift you with a thousand gifts
    that will enable you to live as My Bride
        Bride of the Messiah
        Bride of your Saviour King
        Bride of the Holy Spirit.
I am ready to gift you with graces
    that will enable you to think bridal thoughts
        speak bridal words
        make bridal choices
        do bridal deeds
        understand bridal Scriptures
            and enter bridal worship.

I am ready to pour out graces
    that will enable you to love the universal bride
    with My love, with My compassion,
        with My forgiveness.
This means loving the Bride that is still sleeping
    the Bride that is still rebelling.
This means loving with My love
    the Bride that is still so unlovely
    and so unready for My coming.
I am ready to gift you with My love for the Bride,
    your church with all of its spots and wrinkles.

Tell My Bride that
I, your Bridegroom, am in control.
I am in the process of doing
       all that needs to be done.
All that I said that I would do I will do!
You can trust Me to ready My Bride
       for My coming.
You are not alone.
I am with you doing a miraculous
       work in My Bride.
I know what needs to be done
   and I will bring it about
       in My own time
       in My own way
       for the Father's glory!

CHAPTER ELEVEN

LET'S HEAR IT FROM THE DAISIES

"He loves me!"

"He loves me not!"

"He loves me!"

It was one of those days when I needed to hear it from the daisies and I did: "He loves me!"

Flinging my last daisy petal to the azure sky, I kicked up my heels in the sandy beach, and continued my mid-morning prayer walk with: "He loves me! Jesus loves me! My Bridegroom loves me!"

How could I ever doubt the truth of it, I really don't know. I do know that from little on, my left brain was well trained in the truth of God's unconditional love. This petal-plucking game with God was a pure right-brained expression of the reality of God's love for me.

As I settled myself in my favorite prayer sand dune I boldly prayed: "Jesus, say it again! Do You love me? Do

You love Your bride? How about a jewel from Your Word for the Bride I am writing for?''

Gingerly I cut the Scripture and opened to: ''As the Father has loved Me, so I have loved you'' (John 15:9). The Word melted me. Not only does He love me, **but as the Father loves Jesus so Jesus loves me**. As the Father loved Jesus so Jesus loves His bride.

The truth is almost more than we can hold. As the Great I AM, Jehovah Jireh, loved Y'shua, so our Bridegroom loves us. The most we can do is to be still before the truth: As the Father loves Jesus, so Jesus loves me! So Jesus loves us! To infinity—that is how much we are loved by our Bridegroom.

GOD IS LOVE is the heart of the Scripture. Love can only grow as it is responded to. The love of a Shepherd for His sheep, the Divine Physician for the sick, the Redeemer for the redeemed, the Master for the disciples.

For a long time I sat pondering the truth of God's love in all these love relationships. I realized that in all of them God is the Lover and we are the Beloved. Bridal love needs to be accepted and reciprocated. In our relationship with the Bridegroom, if we, who are the Bride are not willing to enter into a Divine romance, love can go nowhere but dry up. When it is reciprocated, the relationship will not only grow, it will soar!

I read some time ago that we make the choice today between being a mystic or a neurotic. A mystic is someone open to intimate knowledge of God and spousal prayer. We come to know God the way a human spouse would know their beloved. The invitation is to everyone whether married, celibate, single, masculine, or feminine. The invitation is to you. The invitation is to me.

All of our relationships with God are temporary and passing except one:

Jesus is the Saviour...we are saved.

Jesus is the Healer...we are healed.

Jesus is the Teacher...we are taught.

Only the relationship of the Bridegroom and the Bride will be eternal...Forever! Throughout eternity Jesus will be the Bridegroom and we will be the Bride.

How urgent and how rewarding it would be for us to enter in and to grow in this relationship that will be ours for all eternity.

Again as I opened Scripture at random, Jesus reassured me in the Song of Songs not only of His love, but of His presence. "Hark, my beloved! Here He comes, springing across the mountains, leaping across the hills. My Bridegroom is like a gazelle or a young stag. Here He stands behind a wall gazing through the windows, peering through the lattices" (Song of Songs 2:8-9; my paraphrase).

Mystics of all ages like John of the Cross, Teresa of Avilla, Francis of Assisi, and Thomas Merton have written volumes on this whimsical Lover who delights in surprising His Beloved. Now we see Him and now He hides again that our desire to see, to hear, and to experience Him may be sharpened and increased.

Babsie Bleasdell from Trinidad tells how the Lord led her in prayer to the Song of Songs. After reading a few pages she exclaimed: "Oh Lord, I see You want a torrid love affair!"

Yes! Our God wants a torrid love affair with His Bride! The same God who emblazoned His Law on the rock of Sinai wants to emblazon His love and the power to love on the heart of His Bride.

We are challenged to love in the Song of Songs 2:11-14: "My Lover speaks, He says to me: 'Arise, My beautiful one, come. See, the winter has passed, the rains are over and gone, the flowers appear on the earth. The time of pruning the vines has come, and the song of the turtledove is heard in our land. Arise My beloved Bride, My beautiful Bride, arise and come. Let Me see you. Let Me hear your voice, for you voice is sweet and you are lovely!'"

"Jesus, You really do want to hear my voice," I prayed.

"I do," He said. "And let's play the game of your life and Mine as we read through the verses from the Song of Songs."

"Fun!" I agreed.

"It is your turn," He said.

"Your love is more delightful than wine; delicate is the fragrance of Your perfume. Your name is as oil poured out, and that is why the maidens love You. Draw me in Your footsteps, let us run. The King has brought me into His rooms; You will be our joy and our gladness. We shall praise Your love above wine; how right it is to love you" (Song of Songs 1:2-4).

"How beautiful You are, My love, how beautiful You are! How beautiful you are, My beloved, and how delightful!" (Song of Songs 1:15-16).

"As an apple tree among the trees of the orchard, so is My Beloved among the young men. He has taken me to His banquet hall, and the banner He raises over me is love" (Song of Songs 2:3-4).

As I shifted positions on the sand dune it was easy to picture a banner of love in place of a beach umbrella. I began to hum the old tune and Jesus began to sing a new parody:

I am the Bridegroom and you are the Bride
the banner over us is love.
You are My joy, My dance, and My song
the banner over us is love.

I love it. The improvised verses went on and on. "Jesus, if only the whole world could experience You as I do today," I prayed.

"Tell them," He said:

I would love to take each one of you aside
    to court you for three months
    to separate you from the world around you
    to bring you into a deep, deep realization
    that I am your Bridegroom
        and you are My Bride!

I will be your Bridegroom
    and you will be My Bride
        for all eternity.
How I would love to take time
    to be with each of you
        as a bridegroom is with his bride
    to listen to the desires of your heart
        for not just one day or thirty days
        but for three times thirty days.

How I would love to speak to your heart
    that I might reveal to you Who I am
        and to be for you the great I AM!

How I would love to hold you
    close to My heart for ninety days.
But since I cannot do that for each of you
    I have done it for Franny, My Bride.
I have called her that I might give to you
    an inspired series of messages
    that you may understand who you are as
            My Bride
    and Who it is Who loves you.
How I would love to spend a season of time
    with each one of you
    that I might woo you into a deeper love
        and a richer love union.

I desire to share with you the vision
   of the times in which you are living.
You are living in the time of the
   Coming of the Bridegroom.
I am coming and I am coming soon!

Have you ever thought that on a day like today
         a twenty-four hour day
         a day when the sun rises
            in the early morning
            and sets late at night
         a day in which you will eat breakfast
               dinner and perhaps an evening meal
on a day like that
   I, your Bridegroom will come to get you?

I will have the word from My Father
   "Son, it is the time! Go for Your Bride!"

On that day I will come for you, My Bride!
I will take you to Myself into the kingdom
         of My Father.
   On a day like today
         and an hour like this hour...
         I WILL COME!

CHAPTER TWELVE

YOU RAVISH MY HEART

You ravish My heart, My promised Bride
You ravish My heart!
This day I invite you into the garden of My heart.
It is there that I would teach you
   what it is to be yielded to My love.
It is there that I would court you
   that you may know how much I love you
   and desire to call you to Myself.

I love you! I love you! I love you!
   You cannot hear these words too often
   for they hold the truth that will transform you
   into the beautiful, perfect, radiant Bride
     that I call you to be.
I, your Bridegroom,
cannot hear these words too often from your lips

for they are the cords that bind
      your heart to My heart.
Yes, you know that I love you as your God
   but you need to know that I love you
   with the love of a bridegroom
      for his beloved bride.
I would have you gaze into My heart
and see there the desire I have to belong
      wholly to you
so that you may belong wholly to Me.
I, your Bridegroom, have pledged My love to you
   in good times and bad, for richer or for poorer
   until death do we unite.
In death you will find yourself
   in the arms of your Bridegroom
      forever in the embrace of your God
      forever in the eternal union of Love!

If you only knew how much you are loved.
If you only knew the heart of your Bridegroom
   the desire of the Bridegroom
      to hold you to His heart
   to embrace you just as you are
   to call you into that place
   where I can speak to your heart words of love
   that have been in My heart for all eternity.

How I desire to hold you in My arms of love
   arms that have been nailed to the cross
   that you might know My love for you.

My beautiful Bride
   still drag-racing the highways of the world
   in flight from your Divine Lover
you, who have pursued the pathways of sin
   away from your God
you, who have sought out a thousand things

other than your God to find life and happiness.
Turn from those things
   and find in the arms of your Bridegroom
   all that can bring you happiness
      both now and forevermore.

This day I invite you to stop running from Me
   and to start running toward Me.
In My arms you will come to know peace and rest.
There you will hear words of love
   that you have never allowed yourself to hear.
For the truth of all truths is:
   I, the King of kings and the Lord of lords
   I, who reign in the highest heavens
      and upon earth
   I, who am Love, I AM IN LOVE WITH YOU!

Together let us discover the beauty
      that is within you
   beauty, not unlike
      the beauty within the heart of your God.
You, My Bride,
are a reflection of the unlimited beauty
   of your Creator.
   Of all the created beauty in the world
   there is no beauty like the invisible beauty
      of your soul.

I cannot NOT LOVE YOU, as My Bride.
For this you were created.
For this you were called into eternal existence
that you might share forever
      the life of the Trinity
that you might share My Throne forever
that you might share in the mystery
      of the Eternal Nuptials.

In this is truth hidden from all ages
but revealed
　　to the churches and to you, My Bride.
There will never be a time
　　when you, the Bride, can say "I know it all!"
No matter how learned your mind
　　how sharpened your gifts
there will always be infinitely
　　more for you to know
　　infinitely more for you to experience.

You are living in the marvelous age
　　of the courting of the Bride
　　and the coming of the Bridegroom.
In it you will experience
　　a growing desire to be courted
　　a growing knowledge of what it means
　　　　to be courted by your God.
When you say yes to My courting you
　　You say yes to a personal revelation
　　of My bridal love for you.

I call you this day to grow
　　in a season of love and Divine courtship.
I, your God, am here to love you
　　　　to embrace you
　　　　to hold your hand
　　　　to hold you to My heart.

I call you, My darling Bride,
　　for you are precious in My sight.
You are the darling of My heart.
I give you courage, My courage.
I give you faithfulness, My faithfulness.
I give you love, My love.
You shall be My courageous, faithful, loving Bride!
　　For you have the courage, the faith, and the love

of your Bridegroom pledged to you this day.

I will be for you all that you need Me to be.
I will speak to you and I will not grow weary.
I will no longer be silent.
You will hear the voice of your Bridegroom
    in the stillness of your heart.
            I have loved you from all eternity.
            I will love you for all eternity.
            I am madly in love with you.
            I have died that you might have life
            and know the love of the Bridegroom
            for the Bride for all eternity.

Where else in the world can you find such fidelity?
Where else can you find
    such words of love
    such promises of love
    such love as I offer you this day?
I am the Resurrection and the Life!
You, who believe in My love will never perish!

When you invite Me into the garden of your heart
    I come in
    not to concentrate on things
        not ready for My coming
    but that I might open to you the vistas
        of My love.
When you respond to My love with enthusiasm
        you delight My heart!
Be enthused for the ways I would reveal
        My love to you!
Be enthused for the way I call you
        to celebrate My love!

Not by might, not by power
But by My Spirit, I will effect a massive change

in the depths of your being.
It will be a gentle work
for I am a gentle Lover.

I am also a jealous Lover.
I do not tolerate Baals or idols.
You, the Bride, must make choices
If you choose Light, the works of darkness must go.
If you choose freedom, the unfreedoms must go.
If you choose Me, then all that cannot come
under My lordship must go.
I cannot tolerate a Bride
that straddles the Kingdoms.
It is impossible to follow Me
with one foot in each Kingdom.

If you choose Me, you must be willing
to be obedient to My love.
You can no longer say Yes! No! Yes!
Ask and I will give you the grace
to be My obedient Bride
even as I am the obedient Son of My Father.
This is a gift dear to the heart of your Bridegroom.
I paid the price of My life for it.
Do you want security, My Bride?
Be obedient and you will be secure in Me.
Do you want freedom?
Be obedient and you will know the liberty
of the Bride of God.
You, the Bride, who the Son sets free
will be free indeed
free from the anxiety
of knowing that you are doing
the right thing
of knowing that you are
in the right place
of knowing that you are

using your gifts.
Claim for your gift obedience to your Bridegroom
    and all other gifts will be given to you besides.

Ask to see all the events of your life
    through the eyes of your Bridegroom.
As you see through My eyes you will see
        that there are many things
        that you thought you needed
        that you no longer need
        for your treasure is
in the heart of your Bridegroom.
In My arms you will experience
    what it is to be totally wanted
    and to be totally loved.
In My arms you, the Bride,
    who have known abandonment, will be healed.

Bring Me your pain—
    pain in your subconscious and unconscious
    pain felt in search of your healing.
Bring all your pain and shattered dreams
to the foot of My cross and you will know wholeness.

There is no pain in the heart of the Bride
    that was not first borne
        in the heart of your Bridegroom.
You can never say to Me, your Bridegroom:
    "You do not know what it is to be abandoned."

As My Bride, take your place at the foot of My cross
    and experience My dying for you!
Allow the power of Calvary's earthquake
    to strike the rock
        of all your unfreedoms
        your paralyzed emotions
        your unhealed psyche

your bondage to sin
the effects of generational sin in your life.
Allow the full power of My death
and My resurrection
to set you free!

Know the love of your crucified Bridegroom
and everything else will seem
like so much rubbish!

CHAPTER THIRTEEN

AND IT'S NOT FAR OFF

My Bridegoom is the first born of the dead. All the dead from all the nations, who have fallen asleep in death will be brought to life when my Bridegroom calls forth His Bride. All who have died He will bring forth to the glory of His resurrection. We, the Bride, will be there with Him.

And, it's not far off!

Our Bridegroom will be the judge of all the ages. So we, the Bride, can let go of needing to judge the Bride. Jesus will judge the Bride when He hands over the Kingdom to the Father.

And it's not far off!

We, the Bride, will be there to judge the nations with Him (Rev. 2:26-28). Jesus has promised that He will not judge the world by Himself but will share this task with

His Bride (1 Cor. 6:2).
And it's not far off!

We will be placed at the right hand of the Father together with our Bridegroom. We will inherit the Kingdom prepared for us from the beginning of the world.
And it's not far off!

Knowing this, how can we not begin to dream dreams about what life with Jesus will be like when He takes His seat upon His throne as the most exalted King of all kings and invites us to share His throne forever. "I will give the victor the right to sit with Me on My throne, as I Myself won the victory and took My seat beside My Father on His throne" (Rev. 3:21).

How often we have prayed and sung: "Thy Kingdom Come!" This is the Kingdom that has been coming for almost two thousand years, the Kingdom that the Father has prepared for all eternity. It will finally come in full power and glory! We will inherit it together with our Bridegroom!
And it's not far off!

On one of my pilgrimages to the Holy Land Jesus spoke this word:

Trust the way I am forming My Bride, Jerusalem.
I have worked many miracles in the past
    but there is no miracle equal
    to the miracle that I am working in this
        present day to form My Bride, Jerusalem.
Beyond all the violence and all the pain I AM.
I am still the great I AM.
I am the answer to all that is question.
I am hope for all that is hopeless.
Despite all the darkness and the despair
    My power will prevail.

Victory will be Mine.
Be in awe of the mystery of what I am doing.
Even though you do not understand
   or comprehend it.
For I say to you that all the heavenly court stands
   in awe of what they see happening
   and they continually cry holy, holy, holy.
I say to you, today, what I have said before
   in other times to other peoples.
My holy city, Jerusalem
   will welcome the coming of its Bridegroom.
And it's not far off!

My Bridegroom has forgiven and forgotten all my sins. If He cannot remember them why should I? He has removed them from me, as far as the east is from the west. If He has removed them why should I dig them up? With His blood He has washed away my sins. He has purified me in the bath of water and the power of His Word. I am cleansed! I am purified! I am free!

When the time comes Jesus will present me as a glorious Bride, a holy and immaculate bride without stain or wrinkle or anything of that sort. Not only will He present me but He will present my family, my community, my church, the churches and nations of the world. Jesus our Bridegroom will present the Bride.

And it's not far off!

About seven years ago on one of my ministry journeys to Germany, Jesus gave me this word for the Bride of Germany. In the middle of the first night while I was awake awaiting the adjusting of my "zeitgabars," (my internal time clock,) Jesus spoke:

You do not have to twist My arm
   to do something I not only died for
   but I am dying to do today for My people.

Know that nothing is too much for Me to do
   no miracle is beyond My power to work
   no mind is impossible for Me to change
   no heart is impossible for Me to soften.
For I am God, not you
   and I intend to do a mighty work in your midst
   that may astonish many, including you.
It is not for your mind to comprehend
   much less for your small mind to program
   the vastness of what I am about to effect
      because I love you, My Bride.
I have hearkened to the prayers
   of those who have been calling to Me
   to move mightily in your midst.
I shall move indeed and you shall know
   that I, the Lord your God,
      have been the prime mover.
I have long been waiting for this hour
   planned from all eternity.
Do not fear the results of My moving
   by the power of My Spirit among you
   for it is I, Who am the beginning,
   the end, and all the in-betweens,
   Who move among you converting hearts
      filling them with My Spirit
      and giving them hope
      as I gave hope to the early Church.
I am your hope.
Either you move with Me according to My plan
   and with My measure of power
   or you miss Me.
It is possible to miss the moving of your God.
It is possible to miss My plan for your well being
   in this your day.
Therefore I say to you listen to Me.
Pray and watch for the moving of My Spirit
   and you shall see a mighty visitation of your God

that will give birth in you to a new hope,
a new faith, and a new love for your God.
And it's not far off!

One of the most common prophesies as I moved in
ministry in 1984 across Germany was: "I am loosing My
Resurrection power over the cities and the nation."

The day of the fall of the Berlin Wall I wept. For me it
was an Easter! The stone was rolled back! Jesus, our Risen
Bridegroom, could unify a divided nation!

When it seems the whole world is like Humpty
Dumpty ready for a great fall, what a future full of hope
faces us, the Bride. All power is given to us in heaven and
on earth even as it is given to our Bridegroom. All power
is given to us that we might live in the Kingdom, bring in
the Kingdom, inherit the Kingdom, and be readied for the
everlasting Kingdom. There we shall live and reign forever.

And it's not far off!

Our Bridegroom is the heir for all the nations. He will
gather His Bride from all the nations: the German Bride,
the Spanish Bride, the French Bride, the Italian Bride, the
Polish Bride, the British Bride, the Irish Bride, the Russian
Bride, the Oriental Bride, the Kenyan Bride, the Jewish
Bride, the Canadian Bride, the American Bride. Our
Bridegroom is the heir of all the nations! Not one shall be
missing! He will gather His Bride into the kingdom of His
Father.

And it's not far off!

In Jerusalem I have seen previews of this gathering.
For nine years I have been privileged to gather with growing numbers of Christians, international and interdenominational, for a Christian Celebration of the Jewish
Feast of Tabernacles. In the first year, 1980, there were fifty.
In the following years there were one thousand, three
thousand, four thousand, and finally a leveling off at six

thousand Christians gathered at the Binyanei HaUma Conference Center in Jerusalem to worship Jesus, as Saviour, Lord, and coming King in the full power of the Holy Spirit.

One purpose of the Christian Celebration of the Jewish Feast of Tabernacles is to say to the Jewish people: "We are not here to convert you, but we are here to love you and to support what God is doing in you."

What is God doing? I believe that He is first gathering together His chosen people and then God will pour out His Spirit upon them. I believe that one of the biggest miracles of all times will be a move of God in His chosen people before the year 2000. I believe that we will see it.

And it's not far off!

At the first Christian Celebration of the Feast Rabbi Goren said: "Your presence here with us during the Feast of Tabernacles is to us Jews a sign, that we are close to the Messianic period. For our prophet Zechariah said that during His reign all the nations of the world will come up to celebrate the Feast with us in Jerusalem."

At another gathering Mayor Kolek welcomed us with: "We have a long time tradition among the Jews that when the Gentiles come up to Jerusalem for the Feast, the Messiah is soon to come. We look upon it as a first coming. You look upon it as a second coming. Regardless He is coming!" Three thousand Christians from some forty nations stood up and cheered and cheered and cheered, until one would think the King himself heard it and could no longer delay His coming.

Over the years the Feast of Tabernacle's Celebration has grown in grandeur, pageantry, and worship! Whatever the year's theme, there was always a sense of celebrating the relationship between the Bride and the Bridegroom through Scripture, worship, teaching, dance, and song. "A song shall be heard in the cities of Judah. And in the streets of Jerusalem. The voice of joy and the voice of gladness. The voice of the Bridegroom and the voice of the bride'' (Jer. 33:10-11).

In 1984 one of the nights was themed ''Rehearsal for the Wedding Feast of the Lamb.'' Some three thousand men, as well as women, came in bridal white. Women came with flowers in their hair and men with boutonnieres on their suits; many came with fresh flowers to wave welcome and worship of the coming King. As we moved in profound worship I kept saying to myself: ''It's only a rehearsal!   What will the real Wedding Feast of the Lamb be like?''

Would it not be a shame if our Bridegroom came and we never dreamt dreams or had a rehearsal for the absolutely biggest event of all history, the Wedding Feast of the Lamb!

And it's not far off!

There are many names for the age in which we are living: the Age of the Holy Spirit, the Age of the Renewal, the Renewal of the Renewal, the Age of Signs and Wonders, the Age of Evangelism, the Age of Mercy and Grace, the Age of the Coming of the Bridegroom.

Within us is the power to welcome the Age of the Coming of the Bridegroom with all of its graces, blessings, and power. Or we can deny that the Age of the Coming of the Bridegroom is here because it does not show up on our ''left brained'' computer. It is possible to miss God.

He is not far off!

As Charles Dickens phrased it in the opening of his novel, *Tale of Two Cities*: ''It was the best of times and the worst of times.'' For us it is the best of times since we are living in the time of the fulfilling of God's Word. Many prophetic words given, ten, fifteen and twenty years ago are being fulfilled today. It is the worst of times for we are seeing ''the wicked continue in their wicked way and the depraved in their depravity'' (Rev. 22:11), and the satanic powers rising on every side. All we have to do is watch the news, read *Newsweek* or any newspaper and we know Revelation 22:11 is today's world.

The days of miracles are not past. God is performing a miracle in the sight of the whole world. The miracle is that in spite of all the unrest, world calamities, moral degradation, political upheavals, religious conflicts, violence, poverty, abuses of every sort, God is calling a people into a relationship of bridal love, so that when He comes for His Bride the Bride will be ready.

And it's not far off!

Have you ever stood and looked at yourself in a mirror and proclaimed: "I am the Bride that will be ready when Jesus comes! My lamp will be trimmed! My heart will be ready!"

For anyone living in a Mega city like London, New York, Paris, Madrid, Berlin, Tokyo, Milwaukee, or Chicago, it does not take a Divine revelation to know that the enemy has come in like a flood. Nor does it take any great revelation to know that our Bridegroom God has raised up a standard against him. The question is: Does the enemy have any hold on me, the Bride?

In a prophetic word from *Your Move, God* the Father assures: "Jesus, your divine Bridegroom, will fight for you and stand with you! Stand with Him, as a beautiful young bride. As I call you to be bride, I call the whole Church to be formed into a beautiful, perfect, radiant Bride. I will have for My Son a victorious, faithful, loving, valiant Bride, formed by My own hand, shaped on My own potter's wheel, redeemed by the Blood of My own Son, designed in the heart of your God from all eternity" (p. 37).

And it's not far off!

Be patient, therefore...
   until the coming of the Lord.
See how the farmer awaits
   the precious yield of the soil.
He looks forward to it patiently
   while the soil receives the
winter and the springs rains.
   You, too, must be patient.
Steady your hearts,
   because the coming of the Lord is at hand.
                    (James 5: 7,8).

CHAPTER FOURTEEN

T 'N T

It was one of those T and T (Trial and Testing) days which we all have regardless of our fidelity to prayer, vitamin intake, and Meyer's-Briggs' combination.

By mid-day I had had it! My prayer began: "Lord, I am about ready to climb the walls! Would You please have Your angels take pictures of me climbing the walls of this holy cottage? Waiting on You, God, is not the easiest thing in the world! In fact, today it is bordering on the impossible!"

A part of me wanted to scream, to pound the floor, to escape down the roadway! Anything to get God's attention! I had become so eager to receive the fullness of God's message that unwittingly I had become anxious.

"God, do You realize how many days have gone by? Do You know how few are left?"

God's answer: Silence!

"God, You have given me a lot for Your Bride. Yet somehow I feel that the heart of Your message, I am still to receive. God, what do I do to receive more?"

God's answer: More silence! Profound silence! In capital letters, SILENCE!

"God, is there a word in Your Word that will tell me what is going on?" I cut the Bible to Song of Songs 5:6: "I opened to my Lover—but my Lover had departed, gone. I sought Him but I did not find Him; I called to Him but He did not answer."

"A fine how do you do," I thought. Now what?

"I will believe like I have never believed. I will trust like I have never trusted. I will love like I have never loved." In my prayer I ran all the "bases" hoping for a home run.

In this hour of my being tested and tried, I prayed for a word from *Your Move, God* and opened to page 87:

Are you weary, shaken and chastened?
You shall be strengthened by the
    power of My Spirit
        in your inner person.
You shall be rooted and grounded
    in the knowledge of your Lord Jesus Christ
    and filled with the fullness of your God.
For am I not able to do exceedingly,
    abundantly beyond all that you
        ask or desire?

You have been before Me
    in perseverance and prayer.
You have prayed the Word
    pondered the Word
    claimed the Word
        and stood on the Word.
Now I, your God, will stand on My Word
and bring My Word made flesh

into your flesh.

"Thank you, Jesus! You are here for me in good times and bad, for better or for worse!"

The present of God's presence was beginning to be felt again. Further assurance came from the Scripture reading for the day: "I am the Lord your God, who brought you from the land of Egypt. Open wide your mouth and I will fill it" (Ps. 81:10).

"God," I prayed, "My mouth is opened wide.
                    Fill it!"
God did with a fresh new word:

You are the Bride of the Crucified.
As you share in His sufferings
   you will share in His glory!
What you suffer in this life
   can never be compared
         to the glory yet to come
which is waiting for you, My Bride.
Use these tests and trials
   and you will triumph by the power
   of your Bridegroom who loves you.

"For I am certain that neither death nor life, neither angels nor principalities, neither the present nor the future, nor powers, neither height nor depth nor any other creature, will be able to separate us from the love of God that comes to us in Christ Jesus, our Lord" (Rom. 8:38-39).

In reading 1 Peter 2:21-24 I discovered something about enduring testings and trials. Our Bridegroom suffered for us and left an example for us to follow in His footsteps. He did no wrong, no deceit was found in His mouth. When He was insulted, He returned no insults. When He was made to suffer, He did not counter with threats. Instead our Bridegroom delivered Himself up to the one who judges justly, to the Father. In His own body, our Bridegroom, Jesus, Son of God, Son of the eternal Father, brought our sins to the cross; so that dead to sin, we, the Bride, can live in accord with God's will.

"By His wounds we are healed" (1 Pet. 2:24). By the wounds in the body of our Bridegroom, the Bride is healed. In my ministry I have seen every kind of healing spoken of in the Scriptures except the raising from the dead. I believe that as we grow in this bridal love for Jesus and experience His bridegroom love for us, we will see a multiplication of miracles of every sort.

We may for a time need to suffer the distress of many trials as we move and grow in this relationship with the Bridegroom but that is so "our faith which is more precious than the passing splendor of fire-tried gold, may by its genuineness lead to praise, glory, and honor when Jesus, our Bridegroom appears" (1 Pet. 1:7). These are the words of Peter, the bride who knew what it was to suffer.

Again Jesus speaks to encourage us to "hang in there tough" in our seasons of testings:

My precious Bride,
as you are being tested and tried
I see you growing in beauty.
How can I describe it but to say
     it is indescribable.
How can I compare it but to say
     it is incomparable.
How can I measure it except to say
     it is immeasurable.
More and more I see in you
     the beauty of My Father.

Look at yourself today in the mirror and say:
My Bridegroom says that I am beautiful.
He says my beauty is incomparable.

He says my beauty is immeasurable.
He says my beauty is indescribable.

Look around you and say: Not only am I beautiful
    but the Bride that is my family is beautiful.
The Bride that is my neighbor
        and my church is beautiful!

Spend time thanking your Bridegroom
    for the beauty in the Bride all around you.
Spend time praying for the Bride
    being tested and tried
Spend time thanking your Bridegroom
    for His faithfulness in standing by you
    in your times of tests and trials.

When you see beauty ads on TV you may often wish
that you were as beautiful as what you see.
Know that your inner supernatural beauty
    is greater than any natural beauty
        that you see.

All earthly beauty will perish
    but the beauty that I see in you, My Bride,
    will never fade, will never vanish.
It will only grow more and more beautiful!

"Hear, O son and daughter, and see; turn your ear,
forget your people and your father's house. So shall the
King desire your beauty; for He is your Lord, and you
must worship Him. All glorious is the king's son and
daughter as they enter; their raiment is threaded with
spun gold. In embroidered apparel they are borne in to the
king" (Ps. 45:11,12,14).

If you could see the Bride
that I see across the face of the earth

the Bride that you meet in the grocery store
the Bride that says "God bless you"
    when you sneeze
the Bride that yields to you on the highway
the Bride that is an addict, a victim, an outcast.
All can be part of My corporate Bride
    that I am inviting
        to the eternal Wedding Banquet.

"The kingdom of heaven may be compared to a king who gave a feast for his son's wedding. He sent his servants to call those who had been invited, but they would not come. Next he sent some more servants. 'Tell those who have been invited,' he said, 'that I have my banquet all prepared, my oxen and fattened cattle have been slaughtered, everything is ready. Come to the wedding.' But they were not interested: one went off to his farm, another to his business, and the rest seized his servants, maltreated them and killed them. The king was furious. He dispatched his troops, destroyed those murderers and burnt their town. Then he said to his servants, 'The wedding is ready; but as those who were invited proved to be unworthy, go to the crossroads in the town and invite everyone you can find to the wedding.' So these servants went out on to the roads and collected together everyone they could find, bad and good alike; and the wedding hall was filled with guests" (Matt. 22:1-10).

This is a time of testing and trial
    for anyone who chooses to follow Me.
You are constantly called to make choices
    for the Kingdom of Light
        or the Kingdom of darkness.
To straddle the Kingdoms
    or to walk with one foot in each Kingdom
        has never been possible.

My bride needs to make a choice
   and to live by that choice.
When you say "yes" to the Kingdom of Light
   everything of the Kingdom of darkness
      must go!
When you say "yes" to My bridal love for you
   then all that would deny that love
   distract from that love
   or relegate that love
      to a "back-burner" must go!

It is your relationship with Me
   that is being tried and tested.
The circumstances for each of you may differ
   but the testing is the same.
My eyes are on you in the trials
   and the testings.
Keep your eyes on your Bridegroom
   and you will know victory in your struggles.

It is your heart that is being tested.
You have not chosen Me
   but I have chosen you to be My bride.
Know that I love you through it all.
I am forever with you.

"The trials that you have had to bear are no more than people normally have. You can trust your Bridegroom not to let you be tried beyond your strength, and with any trial He will give you a way out of it and the strength to bear it" (1 Cor. 10:13).

Further we are encouraged by James, the bride, in his first letter to the early Christians: "Count it pure joy when you are involved in every sort of trial. If any of you is without wisdom. Let them ask it from God who gives generously and ungrudgingly to all, and it will be given to them. We must ask in faith, never doubting, for the doubter is like the surf tossed and driven by the wind. A bride of this sort must not expect to receive anything from the Bridegroom. Happy is the bride who holds out to the end through trial! Once proven the Bride will receive the crown of life that the Bridegroom has promised to those who love Him'' (James 1:2, 5-7, 12; my paraphrase).

As I was moving through this T and T season Jesus said to me one day: ''I am more interested **in winning the whole of you than in your winning the whole world for Me**.'' He first said this to David Wilkerson after he had taken a year off from active ministry to wait upon the Lord.

As I was thinking about this Jesus said: ''I know that you are out there to win the Kingdom for Me. But it is more important to remember:

YOU ARE THE KINGDOM!
Your mind is My kingdom.
Your heart is My kingdom.
The whole of you is My kingdom!

Give to Me the whole of you like a Mother Theresa
    and I will give to you the whole of the Kingdom
        dying on the streets of your cities;
        San Francisco, New York, Chicago.
I will give to you the whole of the Kingdom
    that is your loved ones, your church!
The Father desires to give you the Kingdom,
    but desires to give it in His way.

Read again the temptations
    when the devil took Me up
        on a very high mountain
    and displayed before Me
        all the kingdoms of this world.

The devil promised: "All these will I give to You
If You prostrate Yourself in homage before me."
  I responded, "Away with you, Satan!"
Scripture has it: "You shall do homage to the Lord,
  your God. God alone shall you adore.
At that the devil left Me and the angels came
  and waited on Me" (Matt. 4:10).

When it comes to bringing in the Kingdom
learn from your Bridegroom what it means
  to **follow the voice of the Father and**
  to **distinguish the voice of the tempter**.
As you do, the enemy will also leave you
and angels will come to minister to you,
            My Bride.

Angels (friends from Canada and Dartmouth) did
come to minister to me in my desert solitude on June 28.

Two-thirds of my time had been spent. One month
was left to go. They came to rejoice with me for what God
had already done and to pray with me for what was still
to be.
  In the power of the Holy Spirit they ministered to me
God's prophetic word:

Your desert journey was a long one
  at times painful and filled with frustration
    but My hand was upon you.
My hand led you through the desert.
  I am well pleased with you
  I mean to do My powerful work in you.
Fear not, for I shall never abandon you.
  Do not shirk the calling
    that I have given to you
    but keep your eyes fastened on Me.
I have been preparing the way

for what I would do now.
I have been laying the foundation
   clearing away the rubbish
   preparing the way for the "birthing."
Now I am ready to work in the magnificent,
   marvelous, miraculous power of My Spirit.

For this is the time
   this is the place
   this is the vessel I chose to bring forth a work
   that will glorify My Father in heaven.

The time of trial by fire is over.
Now My word will come forth like fire!
   There will be no holding back!

CHAPTER FIFTEEN

YOU, THE DARLING
I HAVE CHOSEN

My darling Bride,
   for you are My darling!
You may not always feel darling
   because I may seem to be distant from you.
You cannot see Me with your physical eyes.
You cannot hear Me with your physical ears
   but I am near you!
I hold you close to My heart.
All your thoughts, your words, your doings,
   your being tested and tried,
I hold close to My heart.
   For you are My darling and I love you!

I love you through all the tests and trials
   of this time of waiting.
I am sorry for the pain.

I am sorry for the loneliness.
It is part of the process.
It is part of the courting.
It is part of your coming to know
    your emptiness
        that you might be filled,
    your loneliness that I might be
        your all in all.

I love you through the grayness of this day
    as well as the sunshine of yesterday
        and the storm clouds of tomorrow.
I love you through the stillness of this night.
    You are very close to Me.
    I am very close to you.

"Hear then, O Jacob, My servant,
    Israel, whom I have chosen.
Thus says the Lord who made you
    your help, who formed you from the womb:
Fear not, O Jacob, My servant,
    the darling whom I have chosen" (Isa. 44:1-2).

Fear not, beloved Bride,
    before you were formed in the womb,
        I knew you.
I loved you.
I chose you to be Bride for My Son, Jesus.
Before you came to birth I consecrated you.
    I knew all about you.
I said: "I want one just like you."
No one else is going to be just like you.
You will be a unique Bride for My Son.
No one will have eyes like yours
              ears like yours
          a mouth like yours
    a heart and hands like yours.

No one will be able to love like you love.
No one will be able to serve like you serve.
No one will come from your background
    or have your combination of circumstances.
No one will be able to surrender YOUR ALL
    to My bridegroom Son.
You are unique in all of history.

Like My prophet Jeremiah, I chose you.
And I will use you
    for your family,
            your neighborhood,
                your church.
You can say: "Oh no, not me!
I do not know how to speak!"
My word to you as to Jeremiah is:
    "Fear not! Do not be afraid!
    I am with you to protect you.
I will put My words into your mouth"
            (Jer. 1:9).

I will put words of love, encouragement,
    wisdom, and knowledge in your mouth.
I will use you as I used My prophets of old
    to speak for Me.
I will use you to call the Bride
    that has not heard about Me
    that does not know Me as Lord, Saviour,
        as Baptizer in the Holy Spirit.
I will use you to share the Good News
    to bring the Bride in
    from the highways and by-ways
    from places of sin and degradation.
I will use you to bring My Bride to repentance
    healing and wholeness.
I will use you to ready My Bride for My coming!
Even as you allow yourself to be used by Me

you will become more and more
     ready for My coming.

With the swiftness and sureness of the wind
     I caress you, My darling Bride.
I have sent forth My winds
     from the four corners of the earth
     to hold you in an embrace of tenderness!
Whether you deserve it or not
     the sweet breath of My breeze comes to you.
Whether you are on the mountaintop
     or in the valley
          the wind of My Spirit breathes new hope,
          new life, new love, new promise into you!
In the wind I send you the breath of My Spirit.
The more you welcome My Spirit, the greater will be
     the warmth of My love awakened in you.
Allow Me to love you
     with the elements created by My Father:
     the earth, the wind, the sunshine, and the rain.

Hear My voice in the sounds of nature
     ever so gently I am whispering to you:
     "Here I am! Here I am!"
Let your heart skip, leap, dance for the abundance
     of your Bridegroom's gifts all around you.
All is gift!

Daily, I call you to the gift of repentance
     that you may experience more and more
     what it means to be My redeemed Bride
     what it means to have your sins removed from you
          as far as the east is from the west.
There is no sin that I have not paid the price for
     or that the redeeming power
     of My blood cannot cover.
Though your sins may have been red as scarlet,

you, My Bride, stand before Me white as snow.

"I have brushed away your offenses like a cloud
  your sins like a mist;
  return to Me, for I have redeemed you.
Raise a glad cry, you heavens;
  the Lord has done this;
  shout, you depths of the earth.
Break forth, you mountains, into song
  you forest, with all your trees.
  For the LORD has redeemed Jacob
and shows His glory through Israel"
        (Isa. 44:21-23).

There is no moment in which My love
  is standing still.
There is no moment in which your love
  is standing still.
I see you growing in love
  and I hear your heart's cry.
There is no moment when you have ceased loving Me.
Even when it is difficult
  when there is nothing there to encourage you
  when all seems dry desert, painful separation
      and endless waiting
I see your love growing!
I see the desire of your heart is to be totally Mine
  even as the desire in My heart
  is to be totally yours!

My darling bride, there is no standing still for you.
We are in the chariot race together!
I see you with winged feet and a winged heart.
Come, My darling Bride, we shall cut new records
  in the race to love and to be loved!

As you moved through this day, I delighted to bring

to your mind a bit of poetry that you wrote when you
were a novice in Religious life:

> "I have not loved my Love enough.
> My days were ever too divided
> Undecided in their loves...
> God, grant someday I may catch up
> I may have loved my Love enough
> My Bridegroom, Jesus!"

You are not there yet
    but you are racing to the goal!
I have given people visions of you on roller skates
    with the words "roll on with Jesus
    Not ahead, not behind,
        just rolling along at My pace!"

One lifetime can hardly be enough
    to experience the love of your Beloved.
That is what eternity is all about.

My Bride, as you love to sing to Me
    know that I love to sing to you
    as you go about your work
    as you drive along your highways
    as you walk the waterfronts of your world
    hear Me singing to you,
        even as you sing to Me.

"I keep falling in love with you
    madly in love with you over and over again.
You get sweeter and sweeter as the days go by
    Oh, what a love between My Bride and I
    I keep falling in love with you
    madly in love with you over and over again!"
        (Author unknown)

The most important thing in your life
  is that you love Me
  and that you allow Me to love you.
Allow Me to love you
  in all the beauty that fills your day
  and in every circumstance of your life.
Allow Me to love you in a thousand ways every day.

Prepare yourself, My Bride, for the things
  that I am preparing for you.
I am preparing not just a place for you
  but I am preparing for you an eternity
    of joy and of bliss!
Think of the most beautiful things
  your eyes have ever seen
  the most enjoyable things that you have ever done.
  These are the things, and far beyond these
  that I am preparing for you, My Bride,
  a thousand, million, trillion surprises.

My Bride, dream dreams of what it will be like
  to be with your Bridegroom forever.
Even as I desire your coming
  I am creating in your heart the desire
  the longing to be forever with Me.

I invite you, My Bride,
  to rest deeper and deeper in My love
  that you may be made whole and holy.
My heart is the place for you
  to become holy as I am holy.
It is the place for you to ask questions
  to be taught what it means to reverence
  and to esteem the Bride you are
  and the Bride that is My chosen people!

You will find Me, not just in the Word

but in the words of the brothers and sisters
    I call you to live with.
    Listen, as I use them to speak My word to you.
Reverence them even as I reverence you.

Indeed, I am with you
but you will never know
        the power of this ''with-ness''
unless you are also with Me.
This is a daily, hourly, minutely choice
    you must take time to be with Me.
I want to walk with you
        choose to walk with Me.
I want to talk with you
        choose to talk with Me.
I want to be one with you
        choose to be one with Me.

I, your Bridegroom,
        choose to reveal the Father to you.
I will speak plainly to you of the Father.
Ask Me to do this and indeed I shall do it!
This is the greatest desire of My heart—
    to reveal the Father's love to you, My Bride.

Before the world was created
    you were in My mind and in My Father's mind.
We called you forth into existence.
We planned for you!
Whatever the circumstances at your birth
    **KNOW that you were totally planned for
        in the Heart of your God.**

There is nothing hidden from My sight.
All things are open.
All are laid bare to the eyes of your Bridegroom.
Do not let this be a fearful thing

but let this be a joyful thing in your life.
Rejoice that your Bridegroom
    sees everything about you.
He knows all the circumstances of your life.
He knows all that is sinful and weak,
    and in need of redemption.
Not only does He know it all
    but He has provided for the redemption
      of it all!

"It is in our Bridegroom and through His blood that we have been redeemed and our sins forgiven, so immeasurably generous is God's favor to us" (Eph. 1:7-8).

Ask Me and I will root out of your life
    all that is the work of the enemy
      for I would have you rooted
        only in My love.
Before you become poor
    you need to become rich with My riches!

"I pray that your Bridegroom will bestow on you gifts in keeping with the riches of His glory. May your Bridegroom strengthen you inwardly through the working of His Spirit. May Christ dwell in your heart through faith, and may charity be the root and foundation of your life. Thus you will be able to grasp fully, with all the holy ones, the Bride, the breadth and length and height and depth of your Bridegroom's love, and experience this love which sur-passes all knowledge, so that you may attain to the fullness of God. To Him whose power now at work in us, the Bride, can do immeasurably more than we can ask or imagine, to Jesus be glory in the church" (Eph. 3:16-20; my paraphrase).

I have compassion upon you, My bride.
I pour out My healing, compassionate love

into your being that you might be set free
from all that is sickness
    and disease in your body
from all that is destruction in your psyche
from all that is bondage, oppression, depression
or even possession by the enemy.

"The Bride, whom the Bridegroom sets free is free indeed" (John 8:36; my paraphrase).

"I will show mercy to whomever I choose: I will have pity on whomever I wish. So it is not a question of a person's willing or doing but of God's mercy" (Rom. 9:15).

As Trinity We speak to you, the Bride.
You are the darling We have chosen.
We love you with every word in the Word.
Your name and "I love you" are written
    as with the blood of your Bridegroom
    across every page of the Scripture.
For love of you We spoke every word!
For love of you We worked every sign and wonder!
Everything created is Our gift of love!
All We ask is that you receive it
    with love and with reverence.
Then it will be for you a means to worship.

CHAPTER SIXTEEN

"ONE PICTURE IS WORTH A THOUSAND WORDS."

With a writing like this what is left unsaid could be more priceless than what is shared. Stored in my heart are countless pictures all worth a thousand words. How can I fittingly share them with you?

This chapter is a small attempt to urge you to go beyond the written word, to take time to sit back before the forth coming pictures and to enter into contemplation of who you are as Bride and who Jesus is as your Bridegroom.

Your God invites you to ponder the mystery in the pictures together with the depths of His word.

Go slow. One picture is worth a thousand words. Hear those words in the depths of your being. Speak them there. Share them. And yes, shout them from the house top! They are good news.

Today the Bridegroom claims **His Bride, the Church,** since Christ has washed her sins away...the Magi hasten with their gifts to the royal wedding; and the wedding guests rejoice for Christ has changed water into wine, alleluia (Antiphon for Feast of the Epiphany).

To Him whose power now at work in us can do immeasureably more than we can ask or imagine—to Him be glory in **the Church, His Bride,** and in Christ Jesus through all generations, world without end. (Eph. 3:21).

I rejoice heartily in the Lord, in my God is the joy of my soul; For God has clothed me with a robe of salvation, and wrapped me in a mantle of justice. Like a bridegroom adorned with a diadem, like a bride bedecked with her jewels. As the earth brings forth it plants, and a garden makes its growth spring up, so will the Lord God make justice and praise spring up before all the nations. For Zion's sake I will not be silent, for Jerusalem's sake I will not be quiet, until her vindication shines forth like the dawn and her victory like a burning torch.

(Isa. 61:10-11; 62:1).

The angel then said to me: "Write this down: Happy are they who have been invited to the wedding feast of the Lamb." The angel continued, "These words are true; they come from God."

Let us be glad and rejoice, and give honour to him: for the marriage of the Lamb is come, and his wife hath made herself ready.

And to her was granted that she should be arrayed in fine linen, clean and white: for the fine linen is the righteousness of saints.

And he saith unto me, Write, Blessed are they which are called unto the marrige supper of the Lamb. And he saith unto me, These are the true sayings of God.

(Rev. 19:7-9).

Then all will see the Son of Man coming in the clouds with great power and glory...Heaven and earth will pass away but My words will not pass. The Lord, Himself will come down from heaven at the word of command, at the sound of the archangel's voice and God's trumpet; and those who have died in Christ will rise first. Then we, the living, the survivors, will be caught up with them in the clouds to meet the Lord in the air. Thenceforth we shall be with the Lord unceasingly. Console one another with this message.

(Mark 13:26,31; 1 Thes. 4:16-17).

CHAPTER SEVENTEEN

A THOUSAND YEARS IS LIKE A DAY

"In the eyes of my Bridegroom one day is as a thousand years, and a thousand years are as a day" (1 Peter 3:8; my paraphrase).

All time stands still when I think of the timelessness of the relationship that I have with my Bridegroom. What is a day? What is an hour that I spend with Him?

"I would rather spend one day in your courts than a thousand elsewhere" (Ps. 84:10). I would rather spend one hour with my Bridegroom than a hundred elsewhere.

Have you ever sat in your prayer time and looked into the eyes, into the heart of your loving Bridegroom? Have you ever absorbed the love that is there just for you? Your Bridegroom invites you today to sit by His side, to look into His eyes, to look into His heart, to spend an hour with Him.

Jesus invites you to lay down all your plans into His nail-scarred hands. Lay them down one by one and talk to Him about them. Some of them He will allow you to pick up again and to work with. Others He will store in His heart. When you lay down your plans, you will be able to pick up His plans, the plans that He has for you, plans to give you a future full of hope. Talk about them, look into His eyes, feel His love, hear Him say:

My Bride,
I am the way, the truth, the life.
There is no way I can deceive you.
There is no way I can lead you on a wrong path.
I am the Way. We will walk it together.
I am the Truth. We will experience it together.
I am your Life. We will live it together.

I woke up one morning singing, "I'm in love, I'm in love, I'm in love with my God" to the tune of "Our God Reigns." I knew this was a song that my Bridegroom was putting on my heart because I am His bride and I am in love. I am ready to do all the foolish things that someone in love does—walk with starry eyes, beating heart, eternal smile.

"Being in love" is nothing compared to living through love. Our personal love relationship with Jesus is a growing thing. Growing seasons do not have the same romantic glow but here is the time for our love to be tested as we say "yes" to the carrying of our personal cross.

When you awaken in the morning hear your Bridegroom's voice inviting, "Come My love, My dove, My beautiful one. Arise and put on Jesus Christ the crucified, whom your soul loves and in whom your heart rejoices."

Listen to His voice, feel His presence. Be with Him from that first awakening and those first thoughts that percolate through your mind even as your first cup of coffee percolates. Let your thoughts be in relation to Him in whom you live and move and have your being. He is as close to you as your next thought, enter into dialogue with it.

"Jesus, do you see what I am thinking this morning?" Hear Him say, "Tell Me about it!"

You tell Him what you are thinking and feeling.

Jesus tells you what He is thinking and feeling. You begin to know that your life is not separate from His. Your life is one with His.

"Your Bridegroom is near. Dismiss all anxiety from your mind. Present your needs to Him in every form of prayer and in petitions full of gratitude. He in turn will supply all your needs fully in a way worthy of His magnificent riches. Then the peace that is beyond all understanding will stand guard over your heart and your mind in Christ Jesus, your Bridegroom" (Phil. 4:4-8; my paraphrase).

"Think of the love that the Father has lavished on you by letting you be called God's children. That is what you are, but what we are to be in the future, as the bride of Jesus, has not yet been revealed. All we know is that when it is revealed, we shall all be like our Bridegroom because we shall see Him as He really is. Surely everyone who entertains this hope must try to be pure as our Bridegroom is pure, to live a holy life, to be holy just as He is holy" (1 John 3:1-3,7; my paraphrase).

Doesn't that inspire you? Doesn't that make your life worth living? Doesn't that give you a future full of hope? Doesn't that make you desire to use all the time that you have left to draw close to Jesus?

Only Jesus can teach you what it means to have Him for a Bridegroom. He will teach you what it means to walk with Him, to talk with Him, to live with Him, to be engaged to Him. This is the courting time. These are the days in which no matter what your circumstances are, your Bridegroom is desiring to court you, to woo you, to win you, to rapture your heart.

Our Bridegroom gave up His life for us. So we too ought to give up our lives for one another. If we are rich enough in this world's goods, and we see one of our brothers or sisters in need, but close our hearts to them, how can the love of our Bridegroom be living in us?

For if we cannot love our brother and sister whom we see, how can we love the Bridegroom whom we do not see? We, the Bride, are called to love one another, for only if we love one another can the love of our Bridegroom be in us.

We know that the Bridegroom lives in us by the Spirit He has given us. Trust not every spirit, but try them to see if they be of God. Every spirit which acknowledges that Jesus Christ has come in the flesh is from God. So when the voice within us tells us to do this or to do that, we can ask that voice, "Do you acknowledge Jesus Christ, my Bridegroom, who has come in the flesh?" If the voice from within us remains strong and firm, then that is the voice to follow" (1 John 4:1-3; my paraphrase).

If the voice fades away, then what we have been asked to do is not from our Bridegroom.

"'Do not despise prophecies,' your Bridegroom says, but test everything and see if it is Jesus who is speaking. Retain what is good, avoid any semblance of evil. May your Bridegroom make you perfect in holiness. May He preserve you whole and entire, spirit, soul, and body. irreproachable at His coming. He who calls us is trustworthy; therefore, He will do it. He will ready us for His coming and we, the Bride will be ready when He comes" (1 Thess. 5:20-23; my paraphrase).

I am remembering a story about my friend, Arlene, who recently went to be with her Bridegroom. On my return from a trip overseas, I phoned her husband, Paul, to check how Arlene was doing. Arlene was down to seventy-eight pounds, dying of cancer, choosing to die at home.

Paul said, "Arlene doesn't have long to be with us. Each day we celebrate the life that she has left. Would you like to talk with her?"

"Arlene, how are you?" I dared to ask.

"I feel so loved. If that's what God is, I'll just die," was her ready response.

I heard in her voice the passionate desire to be with Jesus. "Arlene, one of these days Jesus is going to come as your Bridegroom and elope with you."

"I love it! I love it!" Arlene's enthusiasm was real.

Jesus came a few days later and eloped with His bride.

At her Resurrection service we sang: "When we've been there ten thousand years, bright shining as the sun, we've no less days to sing God's praise than when we first begun" ("Amazing Grace", v. 3).

As the bride is wholly given to her husband, so we, the Bride, can be wholly given to our Bridegroom, Jesus. We can offer our living bodies as a holy sacrifice, truly pleasing to our Bridegroom, not modeling ourselves on the behavior of the world around us, but allowing our behavior to be modeled on the new mind that is given us in Christ Jesus. This is the only way for us to discover the will of God and to know what it is our Bridegroom wants.

"Set your heart on what pertains to higher realms where your Bridegroom is seated at God's right hand. Be intent on things above rather than on things of earth. After all we have died. Our life is hidden now with Christ, our Bridegroom! When He appears, then we shall appear with

Him in glory" (Col. 3:2-4; my paraphrase).

Rejoice with those who rejoice and be sad with those in sorrow. You, who are the Bride, treat everyone with equal kindness. Never be condescending, but make real friends with the poor, especially the Bride that is poor.

Make hospitality for the Bride your special concern. As for those who persecute you, never curse them, but bless them.

"Vengeance is Mine," says your Bridegroom. "I will pay those back who do evil." Never try to get revenge, leave that to your Bridegroom. If your enemies are hungry, "give them food." If they are thirsty, "give them drink," thus, you will heap red hot coals on their heads. Resist evil and conquer it with good. These are the words of your Bridegroom to the Bride in this time of waiting.

"How rich are the depths of our Bridegroom. How deep His wisdom and knowledge, how impossible to penetrate His motives, and to understand His methods. Who could ever know the mind of our Divine Bridegroom, who could ever be His counselor, who could ever give Him anything or lend Him anything? All that exists come from Him. All is by Him and for Him. To Him be glory, forever and ever" (Rom. 11:33-36; my paraphrase).

"My Bridegroom is the image of the invisible God, the first born of all creatures. In Him is everything in heaven and on earth that was created. Things visible and invisible, whether thrones or dominions, principalities or powers, all were created through Him and for Him" (Col. 1:15-16; my paraphrase).

What a way to brag about the Bridegroom of my soul!

"My Bridegroom is before all else that is. In Him everything continues in being. He is the head of the Bride.

He is the beginning, the first-born of the dead, so that primacy may be His in everything. The first place is given to the Bridegroom in everything. What a word to ponder!" (Col. 1:17-18; my paraphrase).

"It pleased my Father to make absolute fullness reside in Jesus, my Bridegroom. In His person everything will be reconciled, both on earth and in the heavens, making peace through the blood of His cross" (Col. 1:19,20; my paraphrase).

I have been blessed time and again as I have led pilgrimages to the Holy Land to be able to stand on Calvary in the very place where almost two thousand years ago our Bridegroom poured out His life making peace through the blood of His cross. I have prayed there that we the Bride would be graced to receive peace through the blood of His cross.

When I first kissed the "holy ground" in Israel, I later wrote in my prayer journal: "Lord, it is so wonderful to be here where You once walked, talked, and worked miracles."

"What do you mean I once did?" Jesus responded, "I am still here today. You will see Me in the eyes of My people. You will serve Me in My people."

Our Bridegroom is very much alive in His Holy Land. Two thousand years here is like a day. We have sensed His presence on the banks of the Jordan River, where John the Baptist pointed Him out as the Lamb of God, the Baptizer in the Holy Spirit. "I baptize you with water but there stands one in your midst who will baptize you with the Holy Spirit and with fire" (Luke 3:16).

Each year as we renewed our Baptismal vows in the Jordan, we prayed that we, the Bride, might know in deeper and deeper ways what it means to be born again of water and the Holy Spirit. We prayed that we might experience the fullness of Ephesians 5:26-27: "That our Bridegroom gave Himself up for His bride, to make His bride holy, to purify her in the bath of water by the power of the Word. To present to Himself a glorious Church holy and immaculate, without stain, wrinkle or anything of that sort.''

Each year as we renewed our Confirmation in the Upper Room, we prayed for a fresh outpouring of the Holy Spirit upon the Bride present and the universal Bride. During this prayer service year after year the power was so strong that almost everyone "rested in the Spirit" as Jesus transformed and endued His Bride with power from on high.

We all know the story. In Cana of Galilee Jesus attended a wedding with His mother and His apostles. It was there He performed His first miracle of turning water into wine. In 1984, we, too, attended a wedding in Cana. Not only did we attend, but our group provided the music for what is believed to be the first U.S. wedding in Cana of Galilee. Bob and Linda Best from St. Rita's, West Allis, were married there.

Here was the place that we prayed over all the couples for the renewal of their marriage vows and the healing of marriages. Here in Cana our pilgrimage groups prayed over me for the writing of We, the Bride. One year Jesus spoke these prophetic words in response:

> Indeed I am pleased that you keep asking
> for my blessing on We, the Bride in this place
> where I worked My first public miracle
> for a bride and a bridegroom
> at the request of My mother.
> "Son, they have no wine," she said.
>
> I am a God of love and of miracles
> and you will see the miracle of Cana
> in your lives and miraculously spread
> across the face of the earth.

Even now I am pouring forth
an anointing of love upon you, My Bride
   so that you will indeed know
   that I have once again saved the ''best wine''
   of My bridal love for you until last.

One of the most memorable of many precious moments in the Holy Land was the day we joined a Spirit-filled German group for our boat ride across the Sea of Galilee. We were so moved with the exchange of stories of what God was doing in Germany and in the States, that we had a heyday with our cameras and tape recorders to capture it all. An international prayer and praise time followed as our boat moved across the Sea of Galilee.

In a moment of quiet Jesus gave this prophetic word:

I smile at you
   with your tape recorders and your cameras
      trying to capture all that I am doing.
No tape recorder, no camera
on the face of the earth
      can begin to capture what I am doing.
It is so far beyond your dreaming, your scheming,
      your comprehending.

As I draw to conclusion the writing of *We, the Bride*, I realize that our Bridegroom may be smiling knowing that I have only begun to capture what He is doing. It is so far beyond our dreaming, our scheming, and our comprehending.

Somewhere in my dreams and schemes, I had always believed that I would receive a special nugget, a ''golden egg,'' that would forever establish us as the bride of Jesus, with a word, a guide, a plan, to follow the Bridegroom wherever He goes.

Surprise! There is no golden nugget, no magic word, no one-way to grow in our bridal relationship with the

King of kings and Lord of lords.

Jesus promises to be for us the golden nugget as we are faithful to our prayer time. **AS WE LIVE IT, HE WILL GIVE IT!** For each of us the journey will be different. For each it will be blessed.

For each of us
Jesus has a new pair of combat boots
in His hand.

For each of us
Jesus has a final word:

"I have chosen you to be My Bride.
All I need is your permission
to meet you where you are at
and I will reveal myself to you
as the Bridegroom of your soul."

Your God invites you to
a moment of prayer:

Lord Jesus Christ, I give you permission to meet me where I am at. I believe in Your unconditional love for me, a sinner. I believe that You are the Son of God and I invite You into my heart as my personal Saviour and the Bridegroom of my soul. Forgive me all my sins and wash me in Your precious blood. Save me and my family. Heal us in body, soul, and spirit. Release in us all the gifts, the power, and the fruit of Your Holy Spirit. Thank You for choosing me to be Your bride. Teach me how to grow in this relationship. I say yes to being Your bride now and forevermore. Amen.

EPILOGUE

Often I have asked, "How can this book come forth from me for I haven't a single new, fresh, wonderful, life-giving idea in my left brain, even though I have had so many marvelous right-brained experiences through retreats, meditations, and conferences seeing the Bride come alive across the world."

I have seen it often and proclaimed it to be true that the preparing of the Bride and the coming of the Bridegroom are the biggest things happening on the face of the earth today. Yet as I sat in my Cape Cod solitude, I knew in the poverty of my being that I did not have a single thing to say to the world of *We, the Bride*. Everything I had known was like ashes in the mouth.

Unless the Lord build the house, unless the Lord write the book, we labor in vain who write it. I prayed for the grace to let God write it.

God has done it.